UNBREAKABLE

THE SPIES WHO CRACKED THE NAZIS' SECRET CODE

ALSO BY REBECCA E. F. BARONE

Race to the Bottom of the Earth: Surviving Antarctica

Mountain of Fire: The Eruption and
Survivors of Mount St. Helens

UNBREAKABLE

THE SPIES WHO CRACKED THE NAZIS' SECRET CODE

REBECCA E. F. BARONE

SQUARE
FISH

HENRY HOLT AND COMPANY

NEW YORK

SQUARE
FISH

An imprint of Macmillan Publishing Group, LLC
120 Broadway, New York, NY 10271 • mackids.com

Our books may be purchased in bulk for promotional, educational, or business use. Please
contact your local bookseller or the Macmillan Corporate and Premium Sales Department at
(800) 221-7945 ext. 5442 or by email at MacmillanSpecialMarkets@macmillan.com.

The Library of Congress has cataloged the hardcover edition as follows:
Names: Barone, Rebecca E. F., author.
Title: Unbreakable: the spies who cracked the Nazis' secret code / Rebecca E. F. Barone.
Description: First edition. | New York : Henry Holt and Company, 2022. | Includes bibliographical
    references and index. | Audience: Ages 10–14 | Audience: Grades 7–9 | Summary: "A nonfiction
    manuscript for young readers about a group of Allied spies and Codebreakers that cracked the
    Nazis' infamous cypher, allowing them to read secret military messages and turn the tide of
    World War II. During WWII, as the Germans waged war, every Nazi plan, every attack, was sent
    over radio. But to the Allies listening in, the messages sounded like gibberish. The communications
    were encoded with a powerful cypher—unless you could unlock the key to Germany's Enigma
    machine. Featuring historical photos, *Unbreakable* tells the story of one of the most dangerous
    wartime code-breaking efforts ever. As Hitler marched his troops across conquered lands and
    deadly "wolfpacks" of German U-Boats prowled the open seas, victory—or defeat—for the Allies
    hinged on their desperate attempts to crack the code. Told in riveting multiple points of view,
    Unbreakable is perfect for fans of *The Boys Who Challenged Hitler* and *The Nazi Hunters*"—Provided
    by publisher.
Identifiers: LCCN 2022016611 | ISBN 9781250814203 (hardcover)
Subjects: LCSH: World War, 1939–1945—Cryptography—Juvenile literature. | Enigma cipher
    system—Juvenile literature. | Cryptographers—Poland—Juvenile literature. | Cryptographers—
    France—Juvenile literature. | Cryptographers—Great Britain—Juvenile literature. | World War,
    1939–1945—Secret service—Juvenile literature.
Classification: LCC D810.C88 B365 2022 | DDC 940.54/8743—dc23/eng/20220428
LC record available at https://lccn.loc.gov/2022016611

Originally published in the United States by Henry Holt and Company
First Square Fish edition, 2024
Book designed by Sarah Kaufman
Maps designed by Samira Iravani
Background images on part openers used under license by Shutterstock
Square Fish logo designed by Filomena Tuosto
Printed in the United States of America by Lakeside Book Company, Harrisonburg, Virginia

ISBN 978-1-250-34663-6
1 3 5 7 9 10 8 6 4 2

AR: 7.7 / LEXILE: 1000L

TO MOM, WHO TAUGHT ME TO READ,
AND DAD, WHO TAUGHT ME TO SPEAK

TABLE OF CONTENTS

AUTHOR'S NOTE

DECIPHERING IS THE CORRECT TERM BUT
WE INVARIABLY SPOKE OF DECODING.
—HUGH ALEXANDER

A CODE IS a substitution: replacing one word, letter, number, or symbol with a different word, letter, number, or symbol in order to hide the original's meaning. When spies give each other secret names to hide their true identities, this is a code. A cipher, on the other hand, is a more complex equation of variables and manipulations. This would be like when you and a friend decide to write a note to each other and agree to change all your *a*'s to *b*'s, *b*'s to *c*'s, *c*'s to *d*'s and so on, so that none of the words make sense to anyone but you two.

Most of this story is about ciphers and the ways in which the ciphers were broken, or *deciphered*. Yet, as Hugh Alexander said above, we often slip from the correct to the common.

The terms *code* and *cipher, decode* and *decipher,* as well as *codebreaker, cryptologist, cryptographer,* and *cryptanalyst* are used interchangeably throughout this story.

EUROPE
1928-1939

Bletchley
Park

Berlin

London

Poznań

Warsaw

UK

GERMANY

POLAND

CZECHOSLOVAKIA

Paris

FRANCE

ROMANIA

ITALY

PORTUGAL

SPAIN

PART 1

Gustave Bertrand

Antoni Palluth

Marian Rejewski

Maksymilian Ciężki

Henryk Zygalski

Rodolphe Lemoine

Gwido Langer

Jerzy Różycki

ONE

TRAITOR
1929—Warsaw, Poland

THE BOX ARRIVED on the last Saturday in January.

Business in the Polish customs office went on as usual, the rhythm of sorting and inspecting undisturbed by the heavy package with a German postmark. In fact, the officer in charge had nearly finished when the urgent request came in.

Return it immediately, the German embassy demanded. There had been a mistake. It was a German package, intended for a German recipient. It should never have been sent to Poland. Cease operations and give it back.

Now, *that* made the customs officer pause.

He did not return the box. He opened it.

A polished surface gleamed in the light. Along a hinge in the back, a wood cover opened to reveal something almost like a typewriter. Elevated keys were arranged in three rows along the bottom, each labeled with a letter of the German alphabet.

But that was where the similarity to a typewriter ended.

There was no inked ribbon, no carriage in which to hold paper to type a letter. Instead, the top of the box was filled with small circular windows arranged in three rows identical to the keyboard below; each window contained a single letter printed on translucent material.

If the customs officer pressed a key, instantly, in the top rows, one letter began to glow. As soon as he released the key, the light went out. If he pressed the same letter key again, an entirely different light and letter shone back.

Quickly, the Polish customs officer made a call. Across town, two men secretly working for the Polish cipher agency understood immediately and rushed to the customs office.

Over the next two days and through the next two nights, the men disassembled, examined, and reassembled the machine.

By Monday morning, they had meticulously put every part back into place. They repackaged the machine in the same box and wrapped it in the same brown paper in which it had arrived.

Poland would return German property to Germany, as requested. The delay, inevitable, due simply to the weekend.

No one in Germany suspected a thing.

Enigma in use.

Two years later, Sunday, November 1, 1931—the
German-Belgian border

Hans-Thilo Schmidt rushed through the doors of the Grand Hotel in Verviers, Belgium, two hours late. He never saw the man sitting in the lobby waiting for him.

To this man, Schmidt was an ordinary German of average build, wearing a dark hat and dark coat. Schmidt was red in the face and puffy around the eyes, both traits the man watching him had been expecting. He knew that Schmidt's train was late, and Schmidt sweated and grew flushed as he hurried to make up lost time. Schmidt's puffy eyes had been expected as well. The people this man watched often suffered from sleepless nights. Treason was never an easy decision.

Not that Schmidt would have noticed the man even if he'd been relaxed and alert. Hans-Thilo Schmidt was far from experienced in spy craft. Last June, when he had first decided to trade secrets for money, he simply walked into the French embassy in Berlin. Incredibly, he plainly announced his intent to sell information to the French government. Without cover and without any personal security, he asked whom he should contact in Paris to do so. Somehow, he had neither been arrested by the Germans nor ignored by the French.

Now, five months later, the German Schmidt was about to meet face-to-face with a French intelligence officer. Hans-Thilo was nervous, and he was late.

At the front desk, the receptionist checked Schmidt into a room already reserved for him and handed him an envelope along with his key. He entered the elevator, and as the doors closed in front of him, the man watching him from the lobby saw him rip into the letter, which read "You are expected in suite 31, first floor, at 12 noon."

At precisely noon, as the letter instructed, Schmidt knocked at suite 31.

The door opened into another world where time seemed to slow as an older woman with elegantly styled white hair greeted him and asked him to wait in the comfortable, richly furnished room. Soft music played gently over the radio. An inviting arrangement of liquor and crystal glasses was set out next to a display of fine cigars. Gratefully, Schmidt eased himself into a plush chair.

"Guten Morgen, Herr Schmidt! Hatten sie eine gute Reise?"

Schmidt jumped as an unfamiliar voice boomed at him in German. An immense man with a shaved head came through a doorway, entering the living area through another room in the suite. Round, dark spectacles framed icy blue eyes that pierced Schmidt with an unwavering stare.

"Sit down, please," the man continued. "How are Madame Schmidt and your two children?"

Schmidt, already on edge, tensed more. He was currently living alone, and his wife, son, and daughter were living with his wife's parents.

"I know," the man said, cutting Schmidt off before he had a chance to answer. "You will want to bring your family back together soon and resume a pleasant life. That, of course, depends on you. We will assist you if your cooperation proves fruitful to us."

Taking an offered glass of whiskey, Schmidt sat back down.

The man confronting him became even more serious. "Your resourcefulness last June in Berlin was quite exceptional and effective, Mr. Schmidt. Quite fortunately you happened upon an official of the French embassy who . . . was inconspicuous. What would you have done if he had thought you were an agent provocateur and called the police?"

This pushed Hans-Thilo Schmidt to his limit. "I thought you would understand!" he snapped, defiant. "If you feel this way, my only option is to withdraw. Others will know how to interpret my motivations and the rationale of my propositions."

"Easy now, Mr. Schmidt," the man responded. "We appreciate your initiative and the benefit we can gain from it.

"Let me be frank," the man continued, "my name is Lemoine, and I represent the French Intelligence Bureau."

Rodolphe Lemoine was the top recruiter and handler for the Deuxième Bureau, the branch of French military intelligence charged with keeping an eye on hostile countries. He was an expert at bringing "assets," people with information and secrets that France needed, into agreement.

One of Lemoine's colleagues had described him as "an amazing person who knows as much about how to compromise a minister as he does recruiting a general. He's as much able to get his hands on a safe as acquire a Yugoslavian passport for you in twenty-four hours."

"That is to say," the same colleague had continued, "you must keep your eyes open and ensure you are not ensnared by the undeniable charm of the man." To Lemoine, another person's weakness was a benefit to be exploited, and he used every advantage, both those that were legal and those that were perhaps not.

This world of secrets and spies was, Lemoine felt, a line of work that benefited from a display of opulence. Money spoke of confidence. And confidence made people comfortable. Comfortable enough, Lemoine knew, to betray their country.

Today's meeting was typical of Lemoine's style: the largest suite, in the most expensive hotel, stocked with fine liquor and large cigars.

"You must have undoubtedly understood," Lemoine continued to Hans-Thilo Schmidt, "that we would have already performed a background check on you. Tell me in detail who you are, what you do, and why you are turning to us. . . . But first, would you like another glass of whiskey?"

With a topped-off glass and now a cigar, Schmidt pulled out his identity cards in silence.

SCHMIDT, HANS-THILO
BORN MAY 13, 1888

Occupation: Beamter im höheren Dienst, Chiffrierstelle
[senior civil servant at the German cipher office]

Whiskey before lunch loosened Schmidt's tongue, and he began to speak.

He had not always been poor. His mother had been born a baroness. He had married a wealthy woman, and his in-laws gave him a house and some land just outside of Berlin as a wedding present. But then Germany's economy declined, and the money went with it. Even with a university degree, finding a career as a chemist was impossible as Germans throughout the country all scrambled for jobs and money. His injuries from the First World War eliminated any possibility of a position as a soldier, too.

Hans-Thilo's brother, on the other hand, was quickly rising through the military ranks, and he managed to use his influence to find Hans-Thilo a job as the assistant to the head of the German cipher office. Mostly, Hans-Thilo arranged appointments and kept track of paperwork. Yet he freely came and went through his commander's office. An office that contained a safe.

It was widely known that the Germans had developed a new type of cipher. Not that anyone in Germany had said as much; they didn't need to. It had become obvious the moment the rest of the world had stopped being able to read their transmissions.

For years, nothing had worked to break the new code; they had never seen a cipher like it before. The Germans were using a mechanical device—the Enigma machine—to rearrange letters of a message into an untraceable pattern. The result was a cipher more complex than any before it. No one could break the German Enigma.

Decoding the cipher and accessing all of the political and military intelligence within its messages would give an enormous advantage to anyone opposing Germany. And though there was currently a fragile peace in Europe—it had been over a decade since the end of WWI—signs of war were once again on the horizon.

As a German, Schmidt knew that other countries, France chief among them, were greedy for help from someone on the inside. Someone like him.

The safe in his commander's office held all the information needed to crack the Enigma cipher: manuals, schematics, codebooks, updates, and plans. Hans-Thilo had access to it all, and he was prepared to deliver it to France. For the right price, of course.

Schmidt's salary could never cover anything more than living expenses. And Schmidt had many debts.

"I've been desperate," he said, finally answering Lemoine's question. "Believe me, Mr. Lemoine, the reliability of our Enigma is total, absolute."

Lemoine knew enough to agree.

"Return here next Sunday with as much intelligence as you're able to provide," said Lemoine. "How much do you earn now?"

"Five hundred Reichsmarks a month."

"Here is triple that amount to compensate you for this first assignment, and to assist you with getting back here on Sunday."

The value of the intelligence Schmidt brought next weekend would determine how much he would be paid then.

Rodolphe Lemoine arrived back in Verviers the next Saturday, one day ahead of Schmidt, and he did not come alone. If Schmidt really did bring information as substantial as he had claimed, Lemoine needed to be prepared. This time, the Deuxième Bureau had also sent a photographer as well as a senior officer, Captain Gustave Bertrand.

Bertrand had spent his life around codebreaking, though he couldn't untangle a cipher to save his life. He preferred to learn secrets a more discreet way. By enabling agents and spies, forging alliances, and purchasing foreign codebooks outright, Bertrand helped to break codes without sitting behind a desk. Lemoine had promised him a windfall.

The next morning, they waited. While Lemoine was downstairs, "settled in like a prince, as usual, in suite 31," Bertrand and the photographer stayed in the two other, much smaller and simpler, rooms.

Schmidt was due at nine o'clock.

Finally, at ten, the phone in Bertrand's room rang.

"We apologize for the delay," Lemoine said. "Can you come down?"

Bertrand rushed out, anxious and impatient, while the photographer stayed with the equipment.

Cigar smoke filled the room, and Schmidt again held a glass of whiskey. When Lemoine made introductions, Schmidt bowed to Bertrand. Though Schmidt wore old, worn-out clothes and dingy shoes, Bertrand remembered that "his blue eyes were beautiful, they shone with intelligence."

"Mr. Barsac," Lemoine began, calling Bertrand by his alias, "you are, I believe, going to be satisfied. Mr. Schmidt did not hesitate to entrust us with a few documents."

Schmidt insisted that he had meant to bring more, too. The list of daily settings for the Enigma, called keys, was usually in his commander's safe, "but my chief left it with one of my colleagues for binding, and I dare not ask for it." He promised to bring it next time.

Lemoine handed Bertrand a folder, thick with hundreds of documents. "He will need them back by no later than 3 P.M. in order to catch the train back to Berlin."

Bertrand took the stairs up to his room three at a time. While the photographer recorded every page, Bertrand read the material. Each sheet was marked GEHEIM—SECRET—and for good reason; Schmidt's documents explained exactly how to set up and operate the German army's Enigma machine.

Before he had left the room, Bertrand had pulled Lemoine aside to discuss payment for their newest spy. At first, Bertrand suggested 5,000 Reichsmarks (about $63,000 in 2022), nearly a full year's salary at Schmidt's regular job. Lemoine, sensing just how excited and impressed Bertrand was, immediately doubled the amount, with the same to be paid again if Schmidt continued to bring information. It was an expensive exchange, but everyone walked away from the meeting satisfied.

Lemoine had his spy. Bertrand had his information.

And Schmidt now had a code name: Asché.

Hundreds of stolen documents! More to come! Bertrand returned to the Deuxième Bureau triumphant. Later, he wrote that Schmidt had just provided him with "the thread that would permit us to get to the heart of the Enigma mystery."

But Bertrand had not fully grasped the complexity of Enigma.

Codebreakers at the Deuxième Bureau had already worked for years to translate Enigma messages. Their efforts had met with so little success that one of Bertrand's colleagues summed it up: "Mechanical encryption is impenetrable. Why waste any time on it?"

When Bertrand returned to Paris and handed over the photographs of the manuals, the material did not change the codebreakers' minds. It was secret information, sure, but it wasn't enough to decipher Enigma messages. Schmidt's manuals explained how to encode messages, not how to read anything that had been intercepted. There wasn't even enough information to explain how to re-create the Enigma from scratch. Without an Enigma machine in hand, this new information was useless.

Crushed but not defeated, Bertrand decided to see if the information could help his colleagues in England. He gave the secret documents to the French station of the British intelligence service. The codebreakers there read the assembled set and even sent the photographs to other codebreakers back home in England.

The verdict stood: Schmidt's information was not enough to break Enigma. The English and the French had given up.

But Bertrand knew there was one more country, one more cipher bureau, that was particularly interested in Enigma.

Bertrand began packing for Poland.

TWO

THE STARTING LINE

December 1931—Warsaw, Poland

POLAND HAD TROUBLE brewing on either side. Sandwiched between Germany to the west and the communist threat of the Soviet Union (USSR) to the east, it was imperative that Poland understand what its enemies were thinking and planning.

"The only ones who are truly passionate about these [cryptography] problems are the Poles," Captain Gustave Bertrand later said.

Now, standing in front of the Saxon Palace in Warsaw, holding his diplomatic bag filled with Asché's documents firmly in hand, Bertrand put his last hope in his friends at the Polish cipher office.

At the palace, grand arches and columns framed a courtyard around the Tomb of the Unknown Soldier. Lawns and hedges sprawled beyond the colonnade, joining the two buildings of the Polish General Staff, the highest offices of the Polish armed forces. Inside, Major Gwido Langer was waiting.

Bertrand wore the small half smile of a man prone to keeping secrets; Langer carried himself with the intense, confident posture of a man used to exploiting any weakness.

Twice, while a soldier during the First World War and in the skirmishes that followed, Langer had become a prisoner of war. He had escaped, too, and had trekked hundreds of miles through

Siberia to rejoin his army. Langer's bravery had become apparent during these wars, but so, too, had his grasp of military strategy; he witnessed and understood how decrypting intelligence had changed defeat to victory in key battles. It made such an impression that Langer devoted the rest of his life to ensuring that Poland could break other countries' codes and access their information. By 1929, Langer had become the head of the Polish cipher office—all of Polish counterintelligence that touched codebreaking was under his command.

And now Bertrand said he had something new.

Inside the Saxon Palace, Bertrand pulled out the photographs. He laid Enigma manuals and instructions in front of Langer. Were they really as worthless as the French and British had said?

Langer took one look, and immediately there was "an explosion of amazement and joy," Bertrand remembered. As soon as he collected himself, Langer rushed out of the room and returned with two colleagues.

"This is extraordinary and unexpected!" one of the Polish codebreakers cried.

Bertrand let them have forty-eight hours to examine the documents. Two days later, when the Frenchman returned to the Saxon Palace, Langer and his colleagues were waiting. "They were radiant," remembered Bertrand. "The Schmidt documents were welcomed like manna in the desert."

"Vous avez fait donner l'artillerie lourde!" ["You brought out the big guns!"] Langer said, not mincing words. "This is crucial for the future of our research. We cannot express enough our gratitude."

For his part, though, Bertrand couldn't help but cringe. After all, his own country's supposedly sophisticated, advanced, scientific

Deuxième Bureau had failed to see any advantage to Schmidt's materials.

Langer noticed. "You do not have the same motivations we do," he said graciously. Poland, not France, was Germany's immediate military objective.

As they parted, Langer couldn't help asking for just a bit more.

"If we had access to one or more of the monthly tables reporting the daily modification—even if they were obsolete—we would progress much further and save years of work," he said.

Inwardly, Bertrand blanched. Asché risked enough as it was; to ask him to bring the most sensitive material would put him in even more danger. But Bertrand promised to relay Langer's request to their spy.

As they parted, they agreed to keep talking. Bertrand offered to share any additional information that their spy might provide, and he would inquire specifically about obtaining the manuals and keys Langer requested. In return, Bertrand suggested that any information or breaks in Enigma discovered by the Polish codebreakers would then be shared with France.

It was a promise, Bertrand thought.

It was a proposal, Langer decided.

THREE

THE MACHINE AND THE METHOD

Enigma with machine lid open.
[National Museum of the US Air Force]

THE ENIGMA MACHINE was immensely complicated. Though it was the size and shape of an ordinary typewriter, it was actually an instrument designed to maul coherent messages into incomprehensible clumps of letters.

It all began when an Enigma operator pressed a key on the keyboard.

First, the electrical signal ran from the keyboard through the plugboard (wires on the front of the machine that connected pairs of letters). Then the signal was routed through three rotors and a reflecting drum. The reflecting drum reversed the direction of the electrical signal and sent it back through each of the three rotors, the plugboard, and finally up to the windows at the top of the machine, where it caused a single letter to glow. The original letter typed on the keyboard was now encrypted into a different letter.

What happened next changed everything.

Once the operator released the key he had been pressing, the machine began to transform. Inside, the rotors started to spin. Sometimes only one rotor turned. Sometimes two or all three rotors turned. With every movement, a brand-new electrical path was created.

Letter by letter, an Enigma operator typed in his original message. Letter by letter, the machine twisted and spun to light up encrypted characters, letters that formed words, which were gibberish and meaningless to anyone looking at the new message.

Once the entire message had passed through the machine, the operator sent the encrypted letters over the radio. Far away, a receiving operator tuned his own radio to a certain frequency and listened in.

Now came the problem of decrypting—taking the encoded message and turning it back into readable German. The only way for the receiving operator to do so was to match his own Enigma machine to the sending machine. The rotors, which could be rearranged, had to be in the same order. The inner core and outer shell of each rotor could twist against each other, and these inner and outer parts had to be matched correctly (called the ring setting). Likewise, the starting angle of each whole rotor (inner and outer pieces together), which could be rotated to a different initial position, needed to be the same. The plugboard, too, had to be connected using the same pairs of letters.

Close-up of the three Enigma rotors. The letters around the outside can rotate with respect to the inner wiring of each rotor.
[TedColes via Wikimedia Commons]

3

Enigma plugboard with several pairs of letters connected.
[Bob Lord via Wikimedia Commons]

Once all this setup was complete, the receiving operator could begin typing in the encrypted message. As he did so, letter by letter, the original message was illuminated in the windows.

But if even one setting was off, if there was even one difference between the two Enigma machines, the message could not be deciphered. Instead of German words, the illuminated letters would continue to form words that were utterly meaningless.

Some settings—like the rotor order, the plugboard connections, and the ring setting—were written in daily codebooks provided to each Enigma operator. Other settings, though, like the initial position of each rotor, changed with every message.

The sending operator had to have a way of telling the receiving operator how to set up his machine.

So, before every Enigma transmission, the sending operator would also include an unencrypted preamble to his message. This beginning section included three letters, one for each rotor. These letters explained the starting angle for each rotor. They were called the indicator settings.

The indicator settings were so important that the Enigma operator repeated them in his preamble.

The Germans knew the Enigma messages couldn't be read unless the machines matched perfectly. They didn't want to take the chance that the indicator settings might be lost to static or a miscommunication. So they repeated the settings. But, in doing so, they overlooked a fundamental truth:

Never repeat something that you want kept secret.

The numbers were astronomical.

There were 403,291,461,126,605,635,584,000,000 ways of creating the wiring within the rotors and 7,905,853,580,025 possible connections within the reversing drum alone. As if that wasn't enough, a plugboard with six pairs of connected letters created another 100,391,791,500 possible settings.

An Enigma codebreaker later wrote that "the Germans reasoned, even if the opponent got his hands on one of the military machines, for example, as a result of military action, not knowing the key [daily settings], he still would be unable to read any message."

It certainly seemed like the Germans were right.

FOUR

RECKLESSNESS

1932—the German-Belgian border

BERTRAND HAD HEARD the plea in Langer's voice. The Polish codebreakers needed more information.

But so did everyone else.

Schmidt had quickly become the most valuable spy among all of France's assets. Along with cipher manuals and instructions, he provided a stream of information on German armament (military weapons), troop movements, war games (drills and strategy for coming battles), and military goals.

At one meeting between Schmidt and agents of the Deuxième Bureau in the fall of 1932, Bertrand's supervisor, André Perruche, pulled Schmidt aside. It had taken Perruche all night to photograph the latest stack of documents Schmidt brought, and the information had made the intelligence officer nervous.

"In the long report that you brought, I noticed some information that could only come from a high level of command," said Perruche. "Can you give me the source?"

Schmidt smiled. "It's my brother. Since July 1, he has been the director of the Kriegsakademie [War Academy]. . . . He has learned things that would truly shock you."

Schmidt regularly "borrowed" documents from his brother. In page after page, each report from the military academy told the same story: the Germans were preparing for war.

The information Schmidt brought was so important that Bertrand and Lemoine paid, happily, whenever he requested a rendezvous. But Schmidt put himself at risk every time he brought them secrets.

By the fall of 1932, one year after they had first started meeting, Bertrand and Lemoine had perfected their system for keeping Schmidt safe. Schmidt had shown Lemoine a method of reading invisible ink.

"It is simple and relatively reliable," Lemoine explained. "He has a good background as a chemist. He writes to us between the lines [of a regular letter] with a simple solution of sodium chloride, holding the letter over steam for about 30 seconds and then covering the contents with a starch solution."

Upon receiving a letter from Schmidt, Lemoine would carefully wipe it with a cotton cloth soaked in silver nitrate. He'd press a hot iron against the wet paper, and Schmidt's invisible message requesting the next meeting would suddenly appear.

Then the traveling began. Along the Belgian-German border, Schmidt snaked his way through "an incredible tangle of fields, gardens, and houses," remembered one agent. "Some buildings had their entries in one country and one or more exits in another." From the train station where Schmidt ended his rail journey from Berlin, he then traveled another six miles by tram and foot through four different towns.

"Your route is impeccable, but it's so long," Schmidt once complained to Lemoine.

The distance was both curse and protection. In the event that Schmidt was followed by suspicious German agents, the route would help throw off any potential tails. But the longer Schmidt traveled, the riskier the journey became. He had no access to diplomatic bags (labeled containers that were illegal for a foreign government to search or seize) like Bertrand used at the Saxon Palace in Warsaw. Schmidt carried whatever information he brought.

He always brought information. And Lemoine always paid.

Tens of thousands of marks—the equivalent of hundreds of thousands of dollars in 2022—changed hands. "At this rate," the head of the Deuxième Bureau observed, "[Schmidt] will cost us as much as all of our other informants put together!"

He was worth every penny.

After the first few meetings, though, everyone realized it would not do to have so much cash on hand, and they came up with a better system to pay Schmidt. Schmidt waited at home in Berlin for a postcard, written with a dull message about something trivial, sent through the regular mail. That was his cue. He then went to the post office, showed his ID, and received an envelope waiting there for him. The envelope contained a luggage ticket. At the train station, Schmidt retrieved the bag associated with the ticket. His payment was stuffed inside.

Bertrand and Lemoine did all they could to protect Schmidt where the Deuxième Bureau was involved. But they couldn't protect him from himself.

Schmidt's shabby clothes had vanished, replaced by expensive suits. He took his wife on a six-week vacation to luxury resorts around the Continent. At home, he added rooms to his house, drank expensive wine, and showered his mistresses and girlfriends (there were many) with presents.

Still, even as Schmidt-code-named-Asché began flaunting his newfound wealth and Bertrand and Lemoine worried over his safety, they couldn't deny him more money. He was far too valuable an asset to drop. The Deuxième Bureau would keep on paying him for as long as he brought them information, and they would hide both him and the money as best they could.

But not even Lemoine could keep an eye on Schmidt all the time.

FIVE

THE VIOLENCE OF WORDS
November 8, 1923 to 1932—Munich, Germany

THOUSANDS OF PEOPLE cowered inside the Bürgerbräukeller beer hall when thirty-four-year-old Adolf Hitler raised his gun, fired a single shot into the ceiling, and announced that the hall was surrounded by his followers. The beer hall, a common place in Germany to hear political speeches, was packed that night, full of people waiting to hear from a trio of police, military, and civil service leaders. Suddenly, everyone was focused on Hitler instead.

He took the German leaders to a back room. Together with a famous general from World War I, Hitler convinced the three to turn over leadership of the local government to the National Socialists German Workers' Party, or Nazis. Triumphantly, Hitler reappeared in the still-crowded beer hall and made a speech extolling Nazi ideals. More than two thousand men, most of whom hadn't supported Hitler before the night began, marched out of the beer hall together, intent on overthrowing the rest of the government.

But by the next day, the putsch, or coup, had failed. Instead of seizing power, Hitler was arrested for the crime of high treason.

Yet Hitler's ideas had already spread, and people rallied around him. He was quickly turning into a celebrity, and his trial became a spectacle, serving as a platform for his views. Hitler's speeches in his own defense were reprinted in newspapers around the country, and rather than exposing him as an insurgent and instigator, the trial became a means of gathering more people to his cause. In the end, he was given an incredibly lenient sentence: five years in the modest Landsberg Prison.

Hitler's spacious, comfortably furnished room could hardly be called a jail cell. Visitors came and went at their leisure, often spending time with Hitler unsupervised. On his birthday, Hitler hosted forty people at a party to celebrate. In the end, he only served nine months of his sentence before being released.

But Hitler had done more than just socialize while in prison. For nine months, he wrote.

Across page after page, in his book *Mein Kampf* [*My Struggle*], Hitler spelled out the problems facing the German people, as he saw them. They were suffering from poverty and unemployment. They lived in a country that was reduced from the empire it had once been. Ordinary citizens were bowed down, made to bear the brunt of shame from the German loss in World War I.

It wasn't their fault, Hitler wrote. The German race was a class of people far superior to the rest of the world, he told them. They needed to blame everyone else.

Jews and communists topped his list, but a wide range of races, identities, and ideologies fell under his condemnation.

"All who are not of a good race"—that is, blond-haired and blue-eyed Germans—"are chaff," wrote Hitler. Anyone not of this "pure" race, he claimed, should be eliminated. He made no attempt to hide the horrific measures he was willing to take to ensure this happened: it "must necessarily be a bloody process."

As the German people grew more dissatisfied, Hitler fed them his ideas and gave them races and religions to hate. Slowly, Hitler and the Nazis began to gain seats in the Reichstag, the lower house of the German legislature. By July 1932, the Nazis held more than a third of the seats.

All the while, as he and his followers gathered support, Hitler was brazen about his goals. In one speech, he proclaimed, "Either the enemy walks over our dead bodies or we over theirs!"

From his failed Beer Hall Putsch, Hitler knew that he could not overthrow the government by force. Speeches, not riots, and the votes that pollical rallies brought would steadily help Hitler to find power.

The violence, he promised, would follow.

SIX

A FOUR-CHARACTER ANSWER TO A SIX-WORD QUESTION

1929 to 1932—Poznań to Warsaw, Poland

LANGER NEEDED HELP.

The violent rhetoric rising from Hitler in Germany, directed not only at Jews but at the Polish people just to the east, made it imperative that Poland understand and anticipate what was coming.

But the new, mechanical German cipher—Enigma—would not yield.

With all of the best men at the cipher office trying and failing to break Enigma, Langer went for a different tack. Most codebreakers were linguists, experts who used known traits and characteristics of language to translate intercepted messages. To crack Enigma, Langer knew he would need to bring in people adept with a new set of tools.

Antoni Palluth was a good place to start. Palluth was an expert at miniature electronics and spyware—radios that could fit into the palm of your hand, easily some of the smallest equipment of their day. Palluth had invented them, and he was the one who had to fix them when they broke. Polish spies working behind foreign borders could hardly be expected to take equipment to a local store to be repaired. Instead, Antoni would go. His wife, Jadwiga, would silently grimace as Antoni removed his pistol from the kitchen cabinet and packed it along with his clothes.

Palluth had become a wizard with radios and electronics as a teenager. He had enlisted in the Polish army just after the First World War, and in one of his first posts he met another recruit with a matching passion for radios: Maksymilian Ciężki. Though Palluth and Ciężki were only stationed together for a few weeks, the two began a friendship that would last almost thirty years and change the course of the coming war.

Ciężki became a captain in the army and was promoted to the head of the German section of the Polish cipher office, working directly for Gwido Langer. Palluth left the military and started his own electronics business.

But when a mysterious German package arrived at the Polish customs office—a package that the German embassy seemed too intent on having returned—Ciężki knew who to call. Palluth had been one of the two men who rushed across Warsaw that last Saturday in January 1929.

Both men had tried to solve Enigma's code. Neither got far.

Finally, with even the creative genius of Palluth and Ciężki failing to break the German cipher, Langer was given permission to "seek information and data concerning the possibility of employing professors of mathematics that are fluent in German to do some strictly confidential work." Langer called on the two old friends— Palluth and Ciężki—to find these people.

Twice a week, Ciężki and Palluth rode the train from Warsaw to Poznań University to teach a special course in codebreaking to the men and women who qualified.

In the end, three of their students stood out: Marian Rejewski, Henryk Zygalski, and Jerzy Różycki.

At twenty-seven years old, Marian Rejewski was the oldest member of the group. The humble, mild-mannered man was as far from a spy as could be imagined; he would never dream of the deception necessary. Academics, math, was his life's work.

Henryk Zygalski and Jerzy Różycki, twenty-four and twenty-three years old, were geniuses as well. They had been the best mathematicians in their year.

By 1932, all three were working for Ciężki at the Saxon Palace.

At first, Rejewski, Zygalski, and Różycki didn't work with the Enigma cipher. Alongside other codebreakers working on military intelligence, they were assigned substitution codes and basic manipulations, like the ones that Ciężki and Palluth had taught them in class. They solved these by looking at patterns, using as much of their knowledge of history and psychology as they did of language. It was very little actual math.

Early on at the cipher office, Rejewski, Zygalski, and Różycki puzzled and worked over one particularly troublesome code used by the German navy. As they spent time combing through the coded dialogues between radio operators, it slowly dawned on them that certain letters appeared too often for it to be just coincidence. In fact, the letter *Y* was a fairly uncommon letter in the German alphabet, but in their code, it appeared suspiciously often. It seemed, they noticed, to come up as often as the much more common letter *W* did when writing German words.

They took a closer look, and one exchange between two German operators jumped out: the first word of the dialogue started with *Y*, and then there were five more words after that. The response to this was short, only four characters long. They tried over and over to line up possible plain-word meanings with the coded message, guessing first one idea and then another, fitting potential answers together.

One of the Polish codebreakers began speculating what the four-character response could be: "Maybe it's a year?"

"If so, then what does it refer to? History?" another of the trio replied, always brainstorming possible solutions.

"Probably."

"What question could a code clerk pose on the spur of the moment that his colleague on another ship or at a naval base . . . could answer with a date?"

"What about, 'Wann wurde _____ geboren?' ['When was ____ born?']"

Maybe the four-character response was a year when a famous German was born?

"No, that's no good. [The question] has to be six words."

"Then how about, 'Wann wurde Friedrich der Grosse geboren?' ['When was Frederick the Great born?']"

Every good German knew the answer: 1712.

A four-character answer to a six-word question.

Just like that, the code fell. The Polish codebreakers had figured it out; they had guessed correctly. Decades later, Rejewski would remember that YOPY meant "when" and YWIN, meant "where."

But that was a substitution code, fairly easily mastered. Enigma was far more complicated.

There were no common, frequently used letters in Enigma messages that would signify a repeated word. It wasn't even possible to identify the number of words in any message, because the messages were all transmitted in three- or five-letter groups. Longer words were broken into several parts, and shorter words were combined.

1827 3225XM C1626 W987
SEXTO

H6R 5RH DE C 1346 = 3TLE = 2TL 224 = HUW XNG =
DKRKI CUZAF MNSDC AWXVJ DVZNH DMOZN NWRJC KKJQO
ELWIK XDUUF ECEGN OUNNQ CIIZX FUTKF BTNWI GOECK
CMYUC KTTYB ZMDTU WCNWH OXOFX ERVQW JUCVY PQACQ
EBMXE NOQKF LWRWR LGKXZ BPYWR GQVYG WJDGA QXKVC
MQQJJ PVSLG WFZJZ HHWQG YFCQQ RMVRR QQIDQ QVVIW
LJLBH LHHDI OFWUY JJQGX BWPZ
CCT 2/3 RCWGN
1852 FLC

Enciphered Enigma message. Sets of five-character blocks, instead of words with variable numbers of letters, were used to send all messages.
[US Department of Defense]

Beyond that, the Enigma messages were short, one-way statements, rather than back-and-forth conversations between operators, so Rejewski, Zygalski, and Różycki couldn't use the same tactic they had when cracking the code used by the German navy.

The best codebreakers at the Polish cipher office weren't getting anywhere with Enigma, because their linguistic tools could not solve a mathematical problem. Which was exactly the reason that Marian Rejewski, Henryk Zygalski, and Jerzy Różycki had been hired. It was time to unleash their new techniques on the German Enigma.

SEVEN

AS BY MAGIC

November 1932—Polish cipher bureau, Saxon Palace, Warsaw, Poland

ONE MORNING, CAPTAIN Ciężki walked into the room where Marian Rejewski worked with the other codebreakers. They exchanged a few pleasantries, but Ciężki quickly invited the mathematician into his office, where they could talk privately.

Ciężki closed the door. "Mr. Rejewski, do you have any spare time during the evenings?"

"Yes, indeed, Mr. Captain," Rejewski replied, in the formal way they spoke to one another.

"Good, good . . . I have something which might interest you. In fact, it is something quite difficult: our best men have not got anywhere with it."

"I need not mention, Mr. Rejewski," Ciężki continued, "that nobody else must know about this work, nor must they even know what you are working on."

Ciężki never explained why he gave Rejewski the first chance at breaking Enigma; perhaps because he was the oldest, perhaps he had shown some gift for codebreaking that was apparent only to Ciężki.

"In a staff, and particularly in a cipher bureau, it's not customary to ask questions," Rejewski later wrote.

Rejewski didn't ask why—he just went to work.

"I was . . . given a separate small room in the [general] staff building, and instructed to renew the studies of Enigma abandoned by my predecessors," Rejewski remembered. In the evenings, he covered his new desk with texts of meaningless letters. He had nothing but what the Polish radio officers had overheard and whatever connections his own mind could make.

Back at Poznań University, Rejewski had taken courses in advanced mathematics called permutations. "With normal algebra," a mathematician later explained, "you can divide a number by two and then multiply it by two and you finish up with what you started with. If you tried that sort of thing with an egg, however, you would finish up not with a reconstituted egg but with an urgent need for a saucepan. Manipulating permutations contains the same idea: you have to treat permutations like eggs, since reversing an operation doesn't put you back where you started." And that was the incredibly complex mathematics of Enigma.

Simply having the coded letters—the intercepted radio transmission—was not enough to get meaning from the message. You couldn't start with the end and work backward, as you might be able to with a normal math problem. To make any real progress, Rejewski knew he needed to start at the beginning. He needed an Enigma machine.

A few weeks later, Ciężki came to see him once again.

"Mr. Rejewski, if you would be so kind," Ciężki said, "I should like you to work on this problem in the daytime as well. I'm afraid you will still not be able to discuss the matter with any of your colleagues, though."

Then Ciężki showed Rejewski the box.

Antoni Palluth—one of the few men to have examined an Enigma machine—had managed to replicate the customs-office Enigma from 1929. It was the beginning, the starting point that Rejewski needed.

Meticulously, Rejewski began mathematically tracing the path of electrical signals through the Enigma, assigning variables to each of the rotors and the plugboard, writing equations to represent how changes in one affected the others.

But no matter how he wrote the equations, no matter how good he was at math, no matter how clever, all he could do was chase the equations around and around in circles, always leading back to another unknown.

If only he could find one, just one, pair of letters—coded and decoded—to feed into his system, then the whole maze would tumble down! If he could just get one wall to crack.

Then, "quite unexpectedly ... at just the right moment," Rejewski remembered, "I was given a photocopy of two tables of daily keys for September and October 1932."

Schmidt had stolen a set of keys. He had given them to Lemoine, who had given them to Bertrand, who had given them to Langer, who had given them to Ciężki, who finally put them right where they needed to be—in front of Rejewski.

In January 1933, Rejewski finally had all the information he needed.

Or, rather, "that is how the matter appeared in theory," Rejewski remembered. "In practice, unfortunately, it was otherwise."

Rejewski's equations *should* have generated answers that led to plain German text.

"But they weren't," Rejewski wrote.

Again and again he tried. He checked every equation. He went back over his work. It *should* have come out. He couldn't understand why it wasn't working.

Until he remembered one of his initial guesses.

The Enigma keyboard was laid out in the same way as a typewriter—not in alphabetical order, but in the way that made touch-typing easiest for German-language messages:

QWERTZUIO

ASDFGHJK

PYXCVBNML

Rejewski had assumed that this same order was connected to the rotors: Q to the first electrical terminal, W to the second, E to the third, and so on.

What if he had assumed wrong?

Rejewski decided to try another way. What if the letters were arranged in alphabetical order?

"This time," Rejewski later wrote, "from my pencil, as by magic," the equations finally worked. When the encrypted messages were fed into his Enigma machine, letters appeared that formed German words.

Rejewski had broken the Enigma code, and the Polish men were reading the German Enigma.

Gwido Langer saw it all.

Through the months when Rejewski had toiled with nothing to show for it, Langer and Bertrand had kept meeting. Streams of information about Enigma—all supplied by Hans-Thilo Schmidt—made their way to Warsaw, fueling Rejewski's decryption.

The two intelligence men, the Polish Langer and the French Bertrand, had never directly spoken the terms of their "agreement": papers, keys, and manuals supplied by Bertrand traded for any progress made by the Polish codebreakers, to be supplied by Langer.

Langer had never promised.

And he did not tell Bertrand that they had broken Enigma.

The same month—Berlin, Germany, 300 miles west of Warsaw

Tense negotiations took place through the night. For more than a month, the German president, Paul von Hindenburg, had been trying to resuscitate a dying government.

His people were out of work, hungry, and poor. They read pamphlets blaming their misfortune on the communists and the Jews. Posters, radio ads, and newsreels told them that von Hindenburg's weak government would not help.

The people wanted a strong leader. They wanted Adolf Hitler.

At first, it seemed like Hitler, a man who had once shouted that "a man like me may perish. A man like me may be beaten to death. But a man like me cannot yield!" would rather have total power or none at all. He had threatened that unless all of the cabinet seats of the German government were occupied by the Nazis, then he would have no part in leading the country. All or none.

Finally, though, in the waning hours of night, as daylight began to creep across the sky, Hitler had compromised. He relented and allowed a few powerful seats in the German cabinet to be given to men outside of his control.

It was hoped—by President von Hindenburg, by politicians from other political parties—that these few cabinet positions would be enough to stop the rise of Nazi domination.

It was a gamble. A gift of power in exchange for help reuniting a broken country. Hindenburg bet that, once given, this power could be withdrawn before the Nazi party gained too much influence.

"The history of Hitler is the history of people underestimating him," journalists would later write.

On January 30, 1933, just after 11 A.M., Adolf Hitler was sworn in as chancellor of the German government.

EIGHT

THE GALE

1933—Warsaw, Poland

TENSION RIPPLED THROUGH Germany. Hitler had taken power and promised to lead the country to the Third Reich, a thousand-year reign of the German people. What lengths would he resort to in order to achieve such an end?

To the east, the cryptologists noticed the change. "We had the impression that the Germans had gotten jittery," remembered Rejewski.

Did the Nazis somehow know the Polish military could read Enigma messages? It was "as if [the Germans] sensed intuitively that something had happened," Rejewski worried. Or were the jittery messages just a result of the turmoil in their own country?

Różycki and Zygalski—brought in to work with Rejewski now that he had broken Enigma—didn't have time to question motivations.

Rejewski had shown them the equations he had written and the method he devised to find each day's settings. But finding the right letters to plug into the equations and test each solution required tedious, time-consuming manipulation of the Enigma machine each and every day. Their fingers cracked and their hands bled as they furiously threw the rotors into place, scraping against the rough metal edges, struggling to keep up.

The messages came flooding in. Across Germany, military and civil groups alike began using Enigma to send secure messages. Different groups of users (the civil authorities, the staff of the armed forces, the army, etc.) were called "nets," and each net began using different keys. Rejewski, Różycki, and Zygalski had to break each key for each net individually, every day.

The codebreakers were forbidden to even mention the Enigma to other cipher bureau employees. Their families, of course, were entirely in the dark. Różycki, barely twenty years old when he first met Palluth and Ciężki, would go home, kiss his mother on the cheek, and lament, "My beautiful mother, it's so sad that you'll never be able to be proud of me."

Rejewski, Zygalski, and Różycki worked in back rooms. A thick black curtain was hung in the doorway to separate their section from the other counterintelligence offices. Marked only by a clock above the curtain, they toiled away, breaking the Enigma cipher and undoing every complication that the Germans twisted into the machine.

The men of the "clock room" kept to themselves.

1938—Saxon Palace, Warsaw, Poland

For five years, the three Polish cryptographers steadily kept up with decryption. Rejewski and Różycki both married, but neither of their spouses knew what they really did all day. They kept their work secret.

But there was no way to hide the entire Saxon Palace.

With all of the highest-ranking military and intelligence officials working in the same place, it was an easy target for German spies. Men from the Abwehr, German military intelligence service, strolled by the palace each day, observing who was coming and going, and taking pictures with hidden cameras to send back to Berlin. The Gestapo, the Nazi secret police force, was already feared throughout Germany. If Poland was ever invaded, these men in the Abwehr's pictures would be at the top of the Gestapo's list for arrest. It was too risky to leave codebreakers open to such danger.

Langer's solution was to move his men.

Ten miles outside of Warsaw, tall, dark pine trees filled the Kabaty Woods. Shrouded with snow in the winter and enveloped with a green canopy of oak and beech trees in the summer, the forest concealed many secrets.

As Langer built a fortress of cement walls and tunnels through the trees, Antoni Palluth added antennas, aerials, and radio interception equipment. The giant radio mast, designed to receive signals from as far away as Tehran, Iran, was state-of-the-art equipment that only Palluth's company was prepared to build. Out in the woods, it was farther away from prying eyes than anything in Warsaw could hope to be.

They called Langer's new site Wicher, which means "the Gale."

No one liked it.

When Bertrand visited it, he remarked, "Everything was in concrete bunkers, from the radio station to the cryptologists' offices: this was the brain of the organization, where work went on day and night in silence."

It was ugly and far from the codebreakers' homes in Warsaw. And what's more, the men missed the secret bit of irony that came from looking out their windows at the Saxon Palace. From their offices in

Warsaw, they had been able to see the Tomb of the Unknown Soldier. It had been a small comfort knowing that they were breaking the "unbreakable" German code as they watched Hermann Göring and Joseph Goebbels—leaders of the German Nazi party visiting Poland as foreign dignitaries—lay wreaths in commemoration.

Out in the Gale in the woods, the three Polish cryptographers broke the day into shifts, working around the clock, and reading more than 75 percent of the Enigma messages they received.

But their desperate work consumed them, leaving them bloody and exhausted.

There had to be another way.

And there was.

The Enigma's daily indicator settings, the three letters transmitted in the message preamble, were still sent twice. The Germans hadn't learned: never repeat something that you want kept secret.

Rejewski seized on the weakness. Certain repeated indicator settings formed a pattern, and a machine, he realized, could use these patterns and take hours of work away from the human codebreakers.

By the middle of October 1938, he had designed—and Antoni Palluth had built—a set of six tall boxes with switches down the front and six stacks of rotors twisting around the top. In two hours or less, these six machines could click through all 17,576 possible combinations from a known rotor starting point. They called it the bomba.

A re-creation of Rejewski's bomba.
[the CODEBREAKERS—an international cryptology game]

No one could ever quite remember how the bomba got its name. One guess was that Różycki named it after "a very popular ice-cream dessert called a bomba which [was] round, with chocolate on the outside. The idea for the machine came while [the codebreakers were] eating it," one Polish officer later claimed.

Another, more formidable, guess was that the heavy weights that dropped inside the box sounded like the thud of a bomb.

At almost the same time Rejewski was unveiling his solution, Henryk Zygalski came up with another, silent, one of his own.

Instead of turning the letters over to a machine to solve, Zygalski invented a method to use a series of 156 sheets of specially designed grid papers. Each piece of grid paper was unique, based on patterns of letters that could be produced from a particular arrangement of rotors and starting positions. By punching holes in the sheets as the codebreakers found patterns in a message's encrypted letters, and then arranging the sheets in a certain order, the codebreakers "could calculate the order of the rotors, the setting of their rings, and . . . in other words, the entire cipher key," Rejewski remembered.

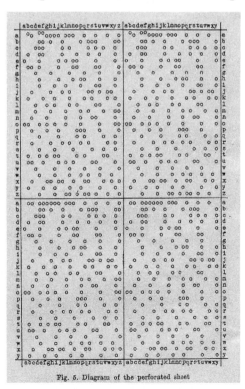

Fig. 5. Diagram of the perforated sheet

Zygalski sheet: by stacking a series of twenty-six sheets and punching holes in each, which corresponded to different rotor positions, Henryk Zygalski was able to create a method to solve for Enigma settings.
[Wikimedia Commons]

They had broken Enigma and had not one but *two* methods of solving for each set of keys! And both the bomba and the Zygalski sheets were well protected in the Kabaty Woods. It almost felt like they could take a breath and relax for a moment.

But the Polish codebreakers weren't the only ones guarding the Enigma secret.

The Germans had more than one way to find out if their code had been broken.

NINE

VERDIER

March 1938—Cologne, Germany

THE GESTAPO CAUGHT Lemoine on March 9, 1938.

He had been operating out of Paris, posing as the head of an industrial company, looking to use this fake position with a fake company to recruit more spies. Under a new code name, Verdier, he had posted job ads in the newspaper. He offered an interview to the most interesting responses at his address: 27 rue de Madrid.

At the interview, as usual, Verdier/Lemoine and his assistant came across as confident, well funded, and well connected. Usually it took some time to "turn" a potential asset. Yet Lemoine knew that money could be very persuasive.

But if potential spies could find their way to Lemoine, so, too, could the Nazis. It was a risk he had been willing to take. Lemoine was not afraid of being arrested; he had been arrested many times before.

Lemoine had built his fortune by cheating. In casinos from Chile and Argentina to London and Berlin, Lemoine picked up "languages, false names, and money with ease," recorded one historian. This method of acquiring wealth, however, came "along with a criminal record for larceny."

Every time he was arrested, he managed to talk his way into a deal, even if it meant swapping a prison sentence for employment with the French intelligence agency. After all, spying wasn't really that different from being a cardsharp. Both were games of deception. And both could make you rich, assuming you didn't mind cheating.

Yet Lemoine had never faced an authority like the Gestapo, and by the spring of 1940, they were on his tail.

The Gestapo had intercepted and traced his letters, and they knew that he was Verdier. And Lemoine. And von König. And Rex. And, originally, Rudolf Stallmann, born 1871 in Berlin, who later moved to France, married a Frenchwoman, and adopted her maiden name as an alias for himself. The Gestapo knew it all, and they wanted to know what Lemoine knew.

They brought him back to Berlin for questioning. In the Gestapo headquarters, two men took turns interrogating him. The first was a blond, tall, powerfully built man. The second, with piercing black eyes, showed Lemoine the thick file they had on him, which detailed almost two decades of illicit activity. Both men gave Lemoine only one option: tell them everything.

After a few days, he was released. Lemoine/Verdier/von König/Rex/Stallmann reported in to the Deuxième Bureau and found intelligence officers going mad at his absence.

"What did you give them?" demanded Paul Paillole, the new head of codebreaking at the French agency.

"Not much, except for a few promises, that with your agreement, I could keep or not keep," Lemoine replied calmly.

To the Gestapo's men, Lemoine had claimed to primarily handle communist assets. From memory, Lemoine had quoted names, dates, codes, and addresses that had been given to him by his communist contacts. All of his information checked out—the details referred to uprisings in Hungary, Czechoslovakia, and Italy that had all occurred just as Lemoine said.

But that didn't mean that Lemoine was helping the Nazis.

"I know from Asché that [the Germans are] already decrypting messages from these countries. The reward would not be of great value," he told Paillole. Lemoine had told his interrogators "secrets" they already knew.

"I can play that game," Lemoine assured the Deuxième Bureau officers.

He hadn't uttered one word against Hans-Thilo Schmidt or the Enigma.

As shocked and concerned as the French intelligence officers were, no one who knew Lemoine could fail to believe that he had pulled off the ruse.

Later, when the French officers discussed it among themselves, their doubt never wavered.

"He had completely fooled them!" one officer said.

"I strongly agree," Major Guy Schlesser, who was overseeing activities with Schmidt and Enigma at the Deuxième Bureau, replied. "We must move past it."

It wouldn't do, though, to leave Lemoine open to further inquiry. Schlesser made the call: "[He] will need to take certain measures: changing his address, not writing indiscriminately, refraining from leaving France, and, above all, severing any and all contact with Asché."

TEN

FAHRENHEIT 451

Spring through fall 1938—Austria

NAZI TROOPS CROSSED the German-Austrian border on March 12, 1938. No one stopped them.

"Any resistance is to be broken mercilessly," Hitler had commanded to more than one hundred thousand soldiers. But the threat had not been necessary; the Nazis had been welcomed. Like the Germans, who faced scarcity and unemployment, Austrians, too, were poor. Many believed that uniting with the Nazis would bring them prosperity.

"As Führer and Chancellor of the German nation and Reich, I announce before history the entry of my homeland into the German empire," declared Hitler, who had been born in Austria, before a cheering audience of hundreds of thousands of people.

The Anschluss, Germany's annexation of Austria, was complete, and barely a shot had been fired.

"What [will come] after . . . Austria?" Langer wrote to Bertrand. "The colonies, Czechoslovakia, us? One can but see that a great deal of explosive material has gathered in Europe. And [what will follow] the explosion?"

Six months later, Langer had his answer.

In September, Hitler ordered the formation of the Sudeten German Freikorps: Czechoslovakian citizens who crossed into Germany, were armed and trained by the Nazi military, and then returned to their country to rise against their government. Many other Czechoslovakians who didn't sign up to fight still considered themselves ethnically German and gave their support for German—and Nazi—rule.

A few weeks later, British prime minister Neville Chamberlain called together European heads of state. They all agreed: let Hitler have part of Czechoslovakia, if it meant forestalling war.

In exchange, Hitler signed a pact, agreeing to promote peace in Europe.

Chamberlain returned to London the same day, triumphantly

British prime minister Neville Chamberlain on his return to England, left, reading from Hitler's signed non-aggression pact.
[Wikimedia Commons]

waving Hitler's agreement with the ink barely dried. From his official residence at No. 10 Downing Street in London, he spoke from a second-story window.

"My good friends," Chamberlain addressed the nation, "this is the second time in our history that there has come back from Germany to Downing Street peace with honor. I believe it is peace for our time."

He did not realize how easily paper can burn.

In the woods outside Warsaw, work went on through the night. It was all too easy for the codebreakers to read what their Enigma messages forecast.

The Germans were getting ready for war.

ELEVEN

TWO MORE ROTORS

December 1938—Kabaty Woods, Poland

THE POLISH CRYPTOGRAPHERS had risen to every challenge. But their luck was about to run out.

On December 15, 1938, the Germans added two more rotors to Enigma's catalogue. There were only three places for rotors within the Enigma machine, but now Enigma operators could choose which three rotors to use from a total of five.

The rotors were the most complex part of the machine, with the wiring inside each rotor different from the others. This meant that the order of the rotors was important. The placement of Rotor I–Rotor II–Rotor III within the Enigma machine would give a different result than Rotor II–Rotor I–Rotor III.

With three rotors, there were only six possible ways to arrange them (I-II-III, I-III-II, II-I-III, II-III-I, III-I-II, III-II-I). But now, with five possible rotors to choose from, there would be an incredible *sixty* possible rotor orders.

Because they understood the wiring, the construction of the rotors wouldn't have been a problem. Marian Rejewski "quickly found the connections within the drums," he remembered. "But the introduction of the new drums raised the number of possible sequences of drums from six to sixty, that is tenfold, and hence also raised tenfold the work of finding the keys."

Instead of six bomba machines to solve the keys, the cryptographers would need ten times as many: sixty bomba machines.

Then, as if the Germans weren't sure that these measures were enough to keep the Enigma machine secure, on January 1, 1939, they started connecting more pairs of letters on the plugboard.

The Zygalski sheets were finished. The Polish cryptographers couldn't make enough to handle the additional rotors. And the manufacture of sixty extra bomba machines would have cost $350,000 (about $6.5 million in 2022). The entire cipher bureau's budget for that year was barely $23,000.

Literally overnight, Enigma messages became unreadable once again. Troop movements, war games, military plans—it all went dark, frozen at what was known the night before December 15, 1938.

It was frightening to be without information. Yet even more chilling was what the change indicated. Outside of the Gale's bunkers, it was beginning to dawn on the rest of Europe as well. The Germans were preparing for war.

Something that even the British had a hard time denying.

TWELVE

WHAT LANGER DIDN'T SAY

Summer 1938—London, England

ALFRED DILLWYN "DILLY" KNOX was getting nowhere.

By 1938, he had already been wrestling with the Enigma problem for two years, and he hadn't read a single message.

It had been almost a decade since British codebreakers had turned down the Deuxième Bureau's offer to share Hans-Thilo Schmidt's information. But the world was different now. Chamberlain had dissected Europe to appease Hitler, and still the monster hungered for more.

Knox was desperate. He badgered his superiors to ask across the English Channel for help. Would the Deuxième Bureau, years later, be willing to share information again?

They asked, and the French quickly replied: yes, they would be glad to help. The more people who were prepared to halt Hitler, the better.

Bertrand did not hold back. Over the course of a year, he sent almost a thousand reports to Knox at the Government Code and Cypher School (GC&CS) such as:

#29—Guide to use of the Enigma cipher machine

#30—Guide to settings of the Enigma cipher machine

#44—Concerning the Enigma cipher machine (Navy model)

Soon Knox's desk was littered with messages, each one written in purple ink, numbered in red, stamped TRÈS SECRET, and sealed with a red flowered monogram. Bertrand's reports were praised as "of very great interest" and "of very considerable value to us."

But it wasn't enough to solve Knox's problems.

Knox was a language man through and through. He had been a codebreaker, and a good one, in the First World War. Afterward, he had happily gone back to his peacetime job at King's College, Cambridge, translating ancient Greek off bits of papyrus.

When the rising tension with Germany called for codebreaking efforts to mount again, Knox answered. But Enigma was way over his head. Two years after he began work on the German cipher, he couldn't make heads or tails of the keyboard connection to the rotors, something that the mathematician Rejewski had solved in a matter of months.

"They were indeed completely in the dark," Bertrand agreed.

The problem was, so were the French. Langer still hadn't told Bertrand that the Polish codebreakers had cracked Enigma. The French had no more idea than their British colleagues of how to read the coded messages.

Knox and Bertrand met once in London in November 1938, but neither could answer the other's questions. They were *both* in the dark.

Bertrand did, however, know that the Polish codebreakers were working with Enigma, even if, to him, they hadn't seemed to make much progress. Perhaps, he thought, together with the British and the French, all three could make some headway on it as a team.

On December 14, 1938, Louis Rivet, at the Deuxième Bureau, wrote to Colonel Stewart Menzies at the British MI6:

Dear Colonel,

After his meeting in London, B [Bertrand] hinted that a collaboration with Warsaw on technical areas could offer common advantages, and asked what you thought: you indicated your consent—leaving him to put things in hand—with the assurance that the sensitivities of each party would be paramount. Accordingly, we thought to bring together representatives of each service in Paris, with a view to putting forward the results of current researches on radio traffic enciphered with the ENIGMA machine used by the WEHRMACHT [Nazi Germany's armed forces]—thinking that this occasion could be the prelude of a deeper collaboration, both in peace and in war. . . .

Bertrand had proposed a meeting: French, British, and Polish codebreakers, together in Paris, sharing their information.

To the GC&CS, Bertrand was formal, asking his superior to send a letter through official channels. But to the Polish cryptographers, with whom he had been working for almost a decade and who he suspected might be further along with Enigma than they admitted, Bertrand was a bit more sly.

It was necessary to get things moving with Enigma, Bertrand told Langer. As Bertrand saw it, there were two options. The first was to use a French agent already embedded in the German military intelligence service, the Abwehr, "to convince our enemy, with supporting evidence, that the messages encrypted by Enigma had been read." This lie, the Deuxième Bureau hoped, would force the Germans to change their encryption system. Perhaps the French would have more luck breaking the next cipher.

The second option was for the French and Polish teams to come together and pool resources with the British.

Langer was caught. The Polish codebreakers had been reading Enigma for six years, and Langer had never told Bertrand. To induce the Germans to change their cipher was unthinkable—it would erase almost a decade of work.

So Langer showed his hand.

Without admitting that they had broken Enigma, "the Poles begged us not to do anything," remembered Paul Paillole, who guessed that they must have a reason for saying so.

Langer agreed to meet in Paris.

January 1939—Paris, France

No one really wanted to be there.

The British representatives were condescending and dismissive. (The cryptologists at the Deuxième Bureau had methods "which were even more clumsy than mine," recorded one British representative.)

The Polish representatives revealed almost nothing. ("*The Poles. Practical knowledge of QWERTZU enigma nil,*" the same British codebreaker wrote.)

The French hosts were simply pleased that their rival department in the Deuxième Bureau, Section du Chiffre, sent a representative for the first day who became so overwhelmed by Enigma's technical details that he didn't bother to return on the second day.

Not much information changed hands during the meeting. Paul Paillole remarked that "from a technical perspective, it was disappointing."

Even Bertrand conceded that "no light was shed on the issue, with neither of the parties wanting to admit [what they knew]." But still, he concluded, "a hope was born out of it."

For all the sniping and posturing, the meeting accomplished its real goal: people met, relationships began to form.

And they agreed on a code. The next time they would meet was when one party stated, "There is something new."

It was all but certain that something new—be it cryptological or political—would happen soon.

THIRTEEN

IL Y A DU NOUVEAU

Spring 1939—Berlin, Germany

ONE YEAR AFTER the Anschluss, and barely six months after he had signed the non-aggression pact with Chamberlain, Hitler moved to take more territory for the German empire. On March 15, 1939, Nazi soldiers entered Prague. They took the port city of Klaipėda in Lithuania a few days later. On the 23rd, they entered the Slovak Republic.

Poland was clearly next.

On April 1, 1939, Britain and France issued pledges to defend Poland. It was a final, desperate attempt to force Hitler to diplomatic, rather than violent, ends.

Instead, Hitler exploded in rage: "I'll cook them in a stew they'll choke on!" he roared.

And yet, even then, the British minister for defense coordination proclaimed to the British people that war "is unlikely."

Hitler, however, knew differently. "The decision remains to attack Poland at the first suitable opportunity," he told his generals in May, preparing them for the violence ahead. "We cannot expect a repetition of Czechoslovakia," which had been annexed largely without violence. "There will be fighting."

Hitler began ripping up pact after treaty after pact. He with-drew from the German-Polish Non-Aggression Pact of 1934 and the Anglo-German Naval Agreement of 1935. Words on sheets of paper—agreements made by supposedly honorable men—meant nothing.

As German tanks and troops moved to line the Polish border, the fragile peace that had marked the end of the First World War finally crumbled. Hitler was poised to begin the violence he had promised, bringing land, money, and power—something new—to the German Reich.

And in the woods just outside of Poland's capital city, Langer telegraphed Bertrand their signal: "Il y a du nouveau." There is something new.

July 1939—Warsaw, Poland

Alastair Denniston (the man in charge of British codebreaking), Dilly Knox, and a naval commander (who "ate and drank too much," Bertrand remembered) arrived in Warsaw on July 24, 1939. They had taken the train across Europe, because they wanted "to see Germany for the last time before all hell broke loose," Knox's colleague later wrote.

Bertrand was waiting for them. He checked them into a hotel and spent the next day entertaining them as guests. Later, he recalled that Knox was "froid, nerveux, ascète" [cold, nervous, and ascetic]. Knox's nerves couldn't handle small talk; all he cared about was seeing what progress the Polish codebreakers had made on Enigma.

Knox got his wish the next morning. They left the hotel at 7 A.M., and drove the dozen miles into the Kabaty Woods. Ciężki and Langer were waiting.

All morning, the Polish officers made grand speeches, boasting about their department. Knox, who hated that kind of thing, sat through it bored and impatient, growing more distrustful of the Polish men with every passing minute.

Then Ciężki said that the Polish men had been reading Enigma for almost seven years.

Denniston watched as Knox sat in "stony silence and was obviously extremely angry about something." It wasn't until that night, when they got in a car to return to the hotel that Knox put a voice to his fury.

"He suddenly let himself go," Denniston remembered, "and, assuming no one [in the car] understood any English, raged and raved that they were lying to us....The whole thing was a fraud he kept on repeating.They never worked it out.They pinched [stole] it years ago and had followed developments as anyone else could but they must have bought it or pinched it."

Their Polish hosts, as well as Bertrand, could, in fact, understand English, and Denniston later sent a remorseful letter to Bertrand, apologizing for Knox's tantrum.

The next morning, their third in Warsaw, Langer brought them out once again to the Gale. He led them downstairs, underneath the cement floors, and around the bunkerlike walls.Then he uncovered one of the boxes sitting in the middle of the room. Everyone knew it on sight.

"Where did you get this from?" asked Bertrand.

"We made it ourselves," responded Langer. "Yes, this is an exact copy of the German machine, built by our cryptanalysts."

It was Zygalski, this time, who stepped forward to demonstrate the Enigma double that Palluth had created and explain how the Polish cryptographers had broken the code.

Immediately after he was finished, Knox turned to ask Rejewski, "Quel est le QWERTZU?" ["Which is the QWERTZU?"]

Knox wanted to know how the keyboard was connected to the rotors. Back in London, Knox had realized that it was not in keyboard order of Q, then W, then E, and so on. But he couldn't puzzle out the correct connections past that.

Rejewski, recalling how his equations had suddenly worked "as by magic" when he changed his own assumption, told Knox that it was simply alphabetical order.

Knox was aghast.

But he couldn't deny that Rejewski was right.

That night, Knox invited Rejewski to his hotel for an impromptu party to celebrate, and the two men chanted together, "Nous avons le QWERTZU; nous marchons ensemble!" ["We have the QWERTZU; we go on together!"]

Later on, Knox told Denniston that "I am fairly clear that Ciężki knows very little about the machine and may try to conceal facts from us." But, he added, "The young men seem very capable and honest."

The Polish and British codebreakers spoke the same language, though they communicated in French that was foreign to both.

After returning home to London, Knox sent each of the three Polish codebreakers a note of thanks for their patience and insight. With each note, he included a gift: a silk scarf showing a winning derby horse crossing a finish line.

July 1939—Paris, France

Bertrand left Warsaw with two heavy diplomatic bags, each containing a replica of the Enigma machine. The first, Bertrand delivered to the Deuxième Bureau in Paris. Then he took a train, a boat, and a plane to hand deliver the other box to GC&CS in London. Knox now had an Enigma double of his own.

Bertrand returned to Paris enthusiastic and amazed. His reception back at the Deuxième Bureau headquarters, however, began on a much different tone.

"If I understand correctly," Guy Schlesser, who was overseeing activities with Schmidt and Enigma at the Deuxième Bureau, spat out, "they've provided you with unusable material and left the effort of making the machine speak to the British and us."

Schlesser was right. The Enigma double from the Polish cryptographers was an old machine with none of the new rotors needed to break the code again.

Yet Bertrand was shocked at the accusation and tried to make Schlesser understand. "Without them we would have no hope of tapping into the Enigma messages for years. You must understand, there would be no hope without the Polish."

"Why is it that for seven years we have been in the dark about what has been going on in Warsaw?" Schlesser demanded.

But Bertrand, more concerned for his professional pride than his personal hurt, defended his colleagues there. He could not, entirely, fault Langer and Ciężki for their secrecy; he might very well have done the same.

"I was sure that privately [Bertrand] deplored their intense reservations," Paul Paillole remembered, attempting to explain Bertrand's reaction to the Polish secrecy. "But today, in possession of what he called the 'miracle machine,' he forgot his complaints and regained his pride."

Enigma was still blacked out—no messages were being read—and the Germans were gathering their strength to mount an attack that would lead to all-out war.

But now, all of the very best codebreakers were poised to strike.

FOURTEEN

HARRY HINSLEY

August 31, 1939—western German countryside

THE WARNING CAME at night.

Harry Hinsley had spent a month of his summer vacation from St. John's College, Cambridge, with his German girlfriend at her parents' house. The thin young man with glasses and longish wavy hair had spent a relaxing August bettering his German language skills and enjoying the beautiful countryside outside Koblenz.

Then, one night, the message came. It was dire and urgent, passed from the police to his girlfriend's parents: "Get him out of the country by tomorrow at the latest."

Hinsley didn't wait. He left that very night.

At the border, the German officers confiscated all of his German money. But they let him go.

In the early dawn hours of September 1, he walked—slowly—across the Kehl bridge as German soldiers leveled guns in one direction and French soldiers aimed across the bridge in the other.

He spent the rest of the night, what was left of it, on a French park bench. He was nearly penniless and far from home, but he had managed to cross the border.

Had the German officers realized how valuable Hinsley was going to become, they never would have let him go.

FIFTEEN

ESCAPE

September 1, 1939—Warsaw, Poland

ON THE SAME day—September 1, 1939—six hundred miles away from Harry Hinsley's park bench on the French-German border, Marian Rejewski was frantic.

Germany had invaded Poland.

German soldiers remove the barrier at the Polish border.
[Wikimedia Commons]

The air raids came first. Planes emblazoned with the black Nazi cross streamed bombs from the sky. From dawn till dusk, they fell. Railroads, factories, roads, and homes were destroyed in an instant. The world shattered, bringing death to cities and causing civilians to flee somewhere, anywhere safer.

German soldiers flowed through the decimated Polish defenses. Days before the invasion of Poland, Hitler had given his orders to his generals: "The object of war is not to reach some given line, but physically to destroy the enemy. That is why I have prepared . . . my 'Death's Head' formations with orders to kill without pity or mercy all men, women, and children of Polish descent or language."

The whole of Warsaw was in terror.

Rejewski had been a young college graduate when he first came to the Enigma problem, but now he was married with two small children. How would his seven-month-old daughter, Janina, survive the hunger and exhaustion of fleeing their home country? But then how could she hope to survive if she stayed?

There was no escape. There was no shelter.

A little way away, Jerzy Różycki and his wife were making the same wrenching decisions. With tears in her eyes, his wife watched as Różycki gave advice to his four-month-old son, masking his grief and distress and speaking to his infant as he could only hope to speak to him one day as an adult.

In the Gale in the Kabaty Woods, chaos burned. Langer had ordered everything destroyed. Nothing could be left behind. No trace of Enigma, no hint that the Polish cryptologists had broken the cipher once and were aiming to do it again. A precious few papers and a few Enigma replicas were loaded onto trucks and taken to the train. But everyone was clamoring for a spot, and no one could properly explain the importance of the heavy green crates coming out of the forest.

The third member of the codebreaking trio, Henryk Zygalski, recorded in his diary on September 5: "Burning of papers, preparation for evacuation."

The next day, simply: "In the evening, departure."

Rejewski, Zygalski, and Różycki left on a train with Langer, Ciężki, and Palluth, aiming to leave the country and escape to Romania. Most brought their families, choosing to escape together rather than face the separation and uncertainty of leaving alone.

Debris from the bombs littered the train tracks. More than once, Zygalski helped clear the way so that the train could continue forward. When air raids came, as they did every day, they climbed out and hid under the train cars until the air cleared.

The train became smaller as cars were ruined. They buried, burned, or destroyed what they could not carry any farther. On September 7, Zygalski's diary records a cryptic note: "Outside Mińsk, a stop in the woods . . ." He did not say what was left behind.

Then, the next day: "Air raids and bombings . . . Captain Zawadzki wounded. During the night, we go through burning Siedlce."

With no other option, they went on. Always south, southeast. To safety.

So they hoped.

The train stopped in Brest-Litovsk, three days after the journey had begun and slightly less than halfway between Warsaw and the Polish border with the USSR. The wives and children would not be taken any farther. Only the all-important codebreakers and the military men would be evacuated from here on out.

Their words, their tears, their embraces were not recorded. The absence of comment in Zygalski's diary was louder than any wail of grief. They could not know it, but one of the three Polish cryptographers would never look upon his wife and child again. They could not know it, but it was certainly what they all feared.

Rejewski, Zygalski, Różycki, Langer, Ciężki, and Palluth were taken with a handful of others too crucial to be left behind. It was cars, buses, and trucks now, "stuffed beyond any normal capacity," Rejewski remembered. Over broken roads and through the countryside. Passing towns battered and burning. Their trucks broke down and ran out of fuel, forcing the codebreakers to abandon vehicles as they became useless.

On September 17, down to one truck and barely half a tank of gas, the Polish group arrived. They crossed a bridge over the Czeremosz River and entered Romania.

Romanian officers confiscated their truck and separated the group. Polish military, including Langer, Ciężki, and Palluth, went one direction. Civilians went another.

For Rejewski, Zygalski, and Różycki, who were not members of the military, their only goals were to survive and to reunite with either the British or French codebreaking teams. Luckily, their quick thinking was not confined to math.

"Befehl ist Befehl!" the Romanians shouted. An order is an order!

"Straight on," Rejewski remembered, "we were supposed to go straight on. So go we did." But their straight path did not end at the refugee camp. In the confusion, the three slipped away.

Vera Atkins, a British spy disguised as a secretary, found them as they left. As a member of the clandestine British Special Operation Executives, she was part of Military Mission Number 4, charged with getting the Polish codebreakers to safety. She managed to secure passage for them on a train, and they rode it all the way to Bucharest.

In the capital city, they found the Polish embassy. But the Polish offices were crammed with people seeking help as they ran from the Germans.

As soon as a Polish official heard that the codebreakers might have British or French friends, he agreed that the three should try another embassy.

They found the British embassy just as a bus of officials was pulling up. "Come back in a few days," they were told. "Well, I took that like the Spanish mañana . . . that is, a rebuff," Rejewski remembered. They would not find any help at the British embassy, either.

They tried the French embassy next. In the lobby, an official asked their purpose.

"Please just tell your superior that we are friends of Bolek." It was a leap of faith, not a prearranged signal, to answer with one of Bertrand's code names. They could only wait to see if it would be recognized.

A moment later, they had their answer.

"Mais oui, messieurs!" the official repeated several times. "Please wait a moment, gentlemen, the colonel will see you just as soon as he has finished speaking with Paris."

For weeks, Bertrand had been anxiously waiting for word about the codebreakers, and soon, the three men were ushered into the colonel's office.

They carried no identification, no travel documents, but the name Bolek and the urgency on the other side of the phone from Paris left no doubt about their travel plans.

"Ah, you have no passports?" the colonel asked. "That's no problem."

A French secretary was dispatched to the overwhelmed Polish embassy, which was "besieged [by] thousands of people . . . who wanted to get passports, too," Rejewski remembered. Through the throngs of people fighting to survive, the secretary fought for an opening.

For almost a year, Polish officials had been preparing for an attack on their homeland by the Germans. Far beneath the official rooms and offices of the embassy, a factory of machines churned out fake identification documents and visas.

The French secretary led the way, asking no further questions of the three and offering no explanation of his underground knowledge. As soon as the Polish cryptographers reached the desk, "they immediately gave us passports," Rejewski remembered. "We wrote out all the information ourselves just as we wanted it [and] they stamped them." Every new document was signed with a fake name; their real identities were sent to Paris in coded dispatches.

A few weeks later—Warsaw, Poland

Jadwiga Palluth, Antoni's wife, had stayed behind. Already an underground resistance had sprung up around Warsaw, and Jadwiga and the Palluth home were at its center.

The house had made it through the air raids. Every single bomb, though the Nazis had targeted it specifically, had missed Antoni's communications factory as well. Somehow the radios, antennas, and wireless equipment stocked at the factory—every bit of which could help the resistance—were left intact. Perilously, so too were the parts for the Enigma doubles.

Everything had to be moved. Without anywhere else to go or any time to destroy it, it had all ended up in the Palluth home.

In a long, wide front hallway—so long and so wide that the young Palluth boy, Jerzy, had learned to ride his bike there—Jadwiga stashed box after box of radio and Enigma equipment as a stream of resistance men emptied the factory of its contents. Every piece of it was now illegal outside of Nazi possession.

The Gestapo were not blind. They saw the trips. It was inevitable they would come.

When the doorbell rang, Jadwiga drew herself straight. She turned to eight-year-old Jerzy and ordered him to stay. "You will watch and listen. It is your duty, to bear witness."

She opened the door, and they came in.

In flawless German, Jadwiga greeted the men, formally and directly. Then, she continued, "In this country, we have the custom that officers remove their hats and sidearms on entering a private house."

"Jawohl, gnädige Frau." ["Yes, good lady."] Obediently, they removed their hats and guns.

But good manners would never conceal the line of boxes standing sentry along the wall.

"Was ist das?" ["What is this?"]

Jadwiga did not so much as flinch. "Since you ask, it is in fact radio equipment."

"What? Did you not know about the decree which required you to surrender all wireless and radio equipment? We could arrest you, and you can be shot!"

"Oh yes. Of course. There is just one problem. Perhaps you would care to lift one of these boxes?"

The German officer did not care to lift one of the boxes, but Jadwiga's point was made.

"Each one of them must weigh about a hundred kilos," she continued. "How am I supposed to take them anywhere? I'm so glad you called, you can take them with you."

"Jawohl, gnädige Frau. We'll send a van round."

It was important, the radio equipment. But these men had a different goal: the man, the mind behind the equipment. They wanted Antoni.

"We need to know where your husband is," the Gestapo officer continued.

Jadwiga looked the officer straight in the eye. "You had better come and sit down. Would you care for some tea? Unfortunately, in view of the situation, I can only offer you herbal tea."

The men did not move. "We need to know: where is your husband?"

"I can only tell you what I know. I last saw him in [early] September. I have had no contact. I assume he must have perished in the war."

"At least you must have some of his belongings."

"Of course. Give me one moment."

Jadwiga left little Jerzy with the men as she walked out of the room. When she came back, she carried a leather-bound book. It had been published before the First World War, and inside, it contained a personal message to Antoni from Kaiser Wilhelm, the last German emperor, who had ceded power in 1918.

"It is one of his most treasured possessions," she said, handing it over, the fearless woman never so much as blinking in the face of the enemy.

The Gestapo men left, and the boxes stayed in the hallway.

September 1939—Bucharest, Romania

It took another two days to get Rejewski, Zygalski, and Różycki out of Bucharest. It was quick, by wartime standards, and all due to their French guardians. When Romanian officials, who had to consent to the Polish men's departures, gave them trouble, the French secretary slipped a bribe into official papers. There were no more arguments after that.

It took them more than twelve hours by train, passing through Belgrade, Zagreb, Croatia, Trieste, and finally reaching Turin, Italy. They were less than two hours' travel away from the French border.

That is, if they weren't arrested on the final leg of their journey.

"Young, in good health, and you haven't served in the army?" A black-uniformed police officer stopped them at the Italian train station, questioning the men. "And you get visas for France so quickly? Extraordinary."

He checked their luggage—it was almost nothing. They had no money, no valuables, no chance of bribing their way through.

But Italy was not at war with Poland. Or with France. In the end, the Italian officer "generously" waved them on.

The alpine air grew sharper. And then, darkness. Through the miles-long tunnel under Mont Cenis, they must have held their breath. At the far side, the train came to a stop.

They were in France.

PART 2

Alan Turing

Harry Hinsley (left) and
Edward Travis (middle)
at Bletchley Park

Gordon Welchman

Paul
Paillole

Karl Dönitz

SIXTEEN

FÜHRER DER U-BOOTE

September 3, 1939—Wilhelmshaven, Germany

"TOTAL GERMANY. REPEAT. TOTAL GERMANY."

Nazi sailors deciphered the signal coming from the British Royal Navy, though it was hardly necessary. Everyone knew what it meant.

Britain had just declared war.

Earlier that morning, Hitler had faced down an ultimatum: cease hostilities in Poland by 11 A.M., or else Britain would retaliate. He had listened as Britain's message was read and then "sat immobile, gazing before him," remembered his interpreter. He did not alter course.

At 11:15 A.M., the British Royal Navy broadcast its signal.

In the German port town of Wilhelmshaven, Commodore Karl Dönitz, head of the U-boat fleet, was conducting his daily briefing when a lieutenant interrupted him, handing him a note with the deciphered message.

Dönitz read it, quickly, crumpled the paper, and threw it down on the table. He jumped up from his chair and began to pace around the room. Back and forth he walked, muttering to himself, "Mein Gott! Also wieder Krieg gegen England!" ["My God! So it's war with England again!"]

Then, abruptly, he ran out.

When he came back a half hour later, he was somber but calm once more. "We know our enemy. We have today the weapon and a leadership that can face up to this enemy. The war will last a long time; but if each does his duty we will win," he told his officers.

It was a line meant to inspire and indicate his complete dedication to the German cause and to Hitler. But in his heart, Dönitz felt only dread. He wasn't alone.

One German naval commander remembered that "we really did not think we could win a war at sea, we saw the situation as quite a desperate one." Even Grand Admiral Erich Raeder, head of the German navy, had lamented only two months earlier that war with England would mean "finis Germaniae"—"the end of Germany," in Latin.

Yet war was here, and Dönitz would face it full-on.

Karl Dönitz was not a tall man, only about average height, neither fat nor thin. But instead of his unremarkable build making him just one of the crowd, his men found him unforgettable.

"He had enormous charisma," remembered one sailor, "and the officers and men were captivated by this charisma."

Dönitz, for his part, was captivated by U-boats. "I was fascinated by that unique spirit of comradeship . . . of a U-boat's crew, where every man's well-being was in the hands of all and where every single man was an indispensable part of the whole," he remembered.

It was good that Dönitz could see the positive side of U-boats, because the reality of working in them was more nightmare than dream.

U-boats, an abbreviation of the German term for "underwater boats," were not true submarines. Diving gave them the ability to hide where surface ships couldn't go, but U-boats traveled and fought on the surface.

And traveling on the surface was nauseating. The shape of the U-boat, which allowed it to pierce the water effortlessly and dive hundreds of feet down to the seafloor, caused it to roll about in the waves. The men were often seasick.

There was only one point of entry and exit to a U-boat: through the conning tower. The oblong column stuck up from the body of the ship, and sailors and officers alike climbed up and down the conning tower ladder to enter and exit.

U-boat 434. The numbers are written on the conning tower, where men would enter and exit the U-boat.
[Thomas Quine]

Then there were the working conditions inside. Though the U-boats were about the size of a Boeing 767 airplane, nearly every space was taken up by pipes, engines, equipment, storage, and weapons. Forty to fifty men were packed into a space so tight that not every man had his own bed; at the start of the deployment, six of the bunks were often used as a storage area for two torpedoes. (The men worked in shifts, so everyone had a place to sleep, eventually.)

There were two toilets for fifty men, but only after food that had initially been stored in the "spare" toilet had been eaten. Until that point, the entire crew used one bathroom. (And any use of the toilet was prohibited when the U-boat was stalking an enemy. The sound of a toilet flush might give the U-boat away.) There certainly weren't any showers—no one bathed for the duration of the tour; they were given cologne instead. Harald Busch, the commander of U-boat *U-576*, described it:

> On board there is no place to be comfortable, stretch your legs, and relax from your strenuous shift, except perhaps the bunk bed, which you have to share with your mates. The work is monotonous and cramped; three times a day you get to wolf down your meal cowered in the tiniest of spaces, then to sleep on an ever soggy bunk bed . . . and soon it is time to report back to duty. There are no showers, no shaves, no getting out of your clothes for the entire time of the trip. But the sailors are proud of their boat and their commander, they are proud to achieve something, proud to play a part in the success. The crew and the commander of a boat form a sworn brotherhood that can even chase the devil out of hell.

The "sworn brotherhood" drew sailors back to their U-boats time and again. Their teamwork, camaraderie, and bravery could be molded into the force the Germans needed to conquer the Atlantic. Dönitz knew it, and all his attention went into making the fleet battle ready.

The highest admirals in the German military were convinced that "very big ships with very big guns," as one historian put it, were the key to winning the war at sea. But Dönitz held fast to his belief in U-boats.

Small, fast U-boats operating in packs could assault enemy supply ships and warships, rising undetected from the deep to surprise and stun their prey. In early 1939, Dönitz called his best and brightest officers to play out war games—strategizing for the different scenarios the enemy might bring.

This practice made clear what Dönitz already believed. It would take three hundred U-boats to win the war: one hundred patrolling the Atlantic, one hundred on their way to or from port, and one hundred in shipyards for refitting and repair. With a year and a half, three hundred U-boats could blockade Britain, starve her people, and force the country to concede.

"I wanted to imbue my crews with enthusiasm and a complete faith in their arm [of the navy] and to instill in them a spirit of selfless readiness to serve. Only those possessed of such a spirit could hope to succeed in the grim realities of submarine warfare. Professional skills alone would not suffice," Dönitz wrote.

Yet, just like surface ships, individual U-boats did not operate alone. Sending and receiving intelligence, new orders, and situation reports required that U-boat crews message other crews, as well as land-based commanders, via radio.

Which meant that nearly every U-boat carried an Enigma machine.

One sailor later remembered, "How safe was the code? . . . We were told that the chances of breaking in were one to one trillion. Today you would say that breaking in was as likely as winning the jackpot in the lottery. But the jackpot exists."

It sounded like enormous odds that the Enigma cipher would be secure, enough to bet heavily on.

Dönitz was going all-in.

SEVENTEEN

PAY HIM

Late fall 1939—Paris, France

HE WAS EITHER a genius or a German agent. Possibly both.

Raffali—no other name was given—had contacted French agents of the Deuxième Bureau, claiming that he could break any German cipher. Even, he said, one that came from a machine. He could, and he would. And he was willing to do so for the French. Assuming, of course, that they paid him what he wanted.

At the Deuxième Bureau, French intelligence agents were mystified. Who was Raffali, and why did he choose that moment, with Poland in chaos and Enigma unreadable, to offer his help? What did he know? And what was he trying to find out?

Was he, even, a spy?

Did the Germans suspect that France, perhaps with the help of allies, was on the verge of reading Enigma? Had the Nazis found out, somehow, that Enigma had been broken before? Were they trying to use Raffali to find out what French cryptographers knew about the code?

Raffali wanted 200,000 francs (about $95,000 in 2022).

Pay him, Bertrand insisted.

Enigma was too precious to lose. If they sent Raffali away

empty-handed, it might signal to France's enemies that they were close to breaking Enigma on their own. The best way to convince Raffali's supporters that France knew nothing was to give him the money.

France needed the Germans to keep using Enigma. It wouldn't hold out against their codebreakers' onslaught of effort forever. Two hundred thousand francs was a lot of money, but having a source of German intelligence was invaluable.

Raffali was paid. And never heard from again.

The same time—25 miles southeast of Paris

Bertrand had been busy.

In the village of Gretz-Armainvilliers, Château de Vignolles, code named PC Bruno, stood against a background of forest and Parisian suburbs.

Château de Vignolles had been a classic, grand manor home: buildings were spread around an expansive park with a guardhouse at the entrance. It had a meadow, grottos, and a pond. The previous occupants had lived a life of aristocratic ease. Clearly one former resident had imagined himself to be quite an artist; the attic was made up like a painter's studio, and many of the interior walls were covered in murals of stylized landscapes.

But that was its former life. Bertrand had gotten his hands on the building and had quickly, efficiently turned it into France's premiere radio intelligence center. French cryptologists as well as Spanish refugee codebreakers crowded the rooms, all working to decipher the myriad codes and ciphers in a multitude of languages that were intercepted and brought to PC Bruno.

(Though Bertrand wasn't above a bit of a joke. The grounds of the château apparently suffered from an infestation of rabbits, and Bertrand created a letterhead that showed bunnies prancing about with the address of PC Bruno listed unhelpfully as "somewhere in France.")

Rejewski, Zygalski, and Różycki arrived less than two months after their escape from Warsaw. They immediately got to work. But not on Enigma.

"At first in France we could not solve Enigma messages, because we had destroyed all our work tools—the perforated sheets and the bombas—before leaving Poland, and without them work was out of the question," Rejewski later remembered.

They carried in their minds the only weapons they had against the most impenetrable cipher: their knowledge and memories.

Bertrand was determined to keep them, and their valuable expertise, safe.

EIGHTEEN

BLETCHLEY PARK

September 1939—Cambridge University, Cambridge, England

HARRY HINSLEY HAD gone back to school. After surviving the terror-filled walk across the bridge between Germany and France, he had hitchhiked to Switzerland and made his way home to England.

Like other young men, he had been given special dispensation to finish his third and final year of undergraduate work, rather than being conscripted into the military. So Hinsley went back to his degree in history.

But school was intolerable.

Every academic concern seemed trivial, and the ways in which people tried to distract themselves were banal at best.

Hinsley would later remember that whenever he met with his advisor that fall, they would quickly read through his latest paper together. "That's very good," his advisor would respond, when Hinsley was finished presenting. "Now would you like to hear me play some music on my harpsichord?"

What was he doing, Hinsley thought over and over! Was he really listening to a harpsichord while war erupted a few hundred miles away? He had *been* there. He had already seen and felt the guns, the hatred that laced the Continent.

He had to do more than simply go to school. He needed to help, somehow.

His solution was already on its way.

Two weeks after the fall term began, Hinsley was summoned to an interview in the offices of the college president. When he arrived, he found Alastair Denniston waiting.

Like Hinsley, Denniston had already seen the war. He had been to the Gale in the Kabaty Woods with Dilly Knox, had spoken to the Polish cryptographers, and seen the Enigma double. He had felt what was coming. And Denniston knew he needed help.

Would Hinsley be willing to take a position in the foreign office, Denniston wanted to know?

Such an offer was so broad as to be almost meaningless— Denniston could have been asking Hinsley to be a diplomat, spy, janitor, mail courier, or a host of other jobs. The work of the foreign office was so classified that Denniston couldn't tell Hinsley what he would be doing until Hinsley accepted the offer and reported for his first day.

Yet Hinsley had his answer ready.

Yes. He would help any way he could.

Three days later, he received a letter instructing him to report to an office in Euston Station, London, on Monday morning.

"It was all done," Hinsley recalled, "with minimum fuss and maximum dispatch."

He only found out where he would truly be headed when his advisor—the same man who had performed for him regularly on the harpsichord—contacted him and said that Hinsley had been recruited by GC&CS.

"I'm going there too," his advisor said, and offered to take

Hinsley not to Euston Station but to the wartime headquarters of GC&CS: Bletchley Park.

Bletchley Park differed in almost every way possible from the stately Château de Vignolles, the PC Bruno home of the French and Polish codebreakers. Bletchley Park was later described as a "nightmare," "hideous," "the Victorian Monstrosity," "irretrievably ugly," "lavatory-Gothic," "inchoate, unfocused, and incomprehensible, not to say indigestible," "a nondescript provincial pile set just outside the most provincial of English towns," and "a dump."

Bletchley Park mansion.
[DeFacto via Wikimedia Commons]

Not only was the architecture awful, but the decoration inside was a mess as well. The central house, the "Victorian Monstrosity," had been so quickly transformed into wartime offices that the commander of Bletchley Park worked in a former nursery with walls still covered in Peter Rabbit wallpaper.

Yet the main house hadn't been the reason why GC&CS chose Bletchley Park as headquarters. Instead, the administrators wanted the space the grounds provided. "Before long," remembered Gordon Welchman, a Bletchley Park codebreaker, the "rose beds and lawn were sacrificed to the much-needed wooden huts." Outside, in nearly a dozen huts spread throughout the grounds, codebreakers did the real work of deciphering messages.

The teams in each hut wrestled with different problems: Hut 6 worked on decrypting the German army/air force Enigma net, Hut 8 attempted to break the German naval Enigma net, and Huts 3 and 4 tried to assemble the bits and pieces of intelligence passed from the other huts into a coherent, useful story. Still more huts and a few outbuildings worked on various other ciphers and codes.

Hut 3 in Bletchley Park, as it stood in 2019.
[TedColes via Wikimedia Commons]

With teams spread around the grounds and administration in the main house, messengers—all girls and young women—biked from building to building. The youngest messenger, fourteen-year-old Mimi Gallilee, later remembered that the messengers' job was "going around delivering the mail, messages—everything of course was in big envelopes—and we weren't even interested in knowing what was inside them."

Absolute secrecy was a given. "You just assumed you'd be shot," remembered one codebreaker.

Mimi Gallilee's sister worked in Hut 10, and though the two lived together and both worked at Bletchley Park for years, Mimi never found out what her sister did. "I never even asked her. She wouldn't have told me anyway," Mimi later remembered.

The rule of silence applied within Bletchley Park as well as without. You never knew who might be a spy or potential traitor ready to funnel information to the Germans in exchange for a big payday. Each hut kept its successes and struggles to itself.

The huts had been built just in time, too. Bletchley Park was quickly filling with some of the best minds in England.

Even as he watched the newcomers arrive, Harry Hinsley couldn't claim to have been the first one there. The "wicked uncles" had already begun making their mark.

NINETEEN

UNCLES

1938 to 1940—Bletchley Park, England

BACK IN 1938, even before he and Dilly Knox had met with Rejewski, Zygalski, and Różycki, Alastair Denniston had realized what was on the way. While the British prime minister might be trying to appease Hitler and stave off war, Denniston began to plan for the inevitable.

Quietly, he began asking around, mostly through word of mouth, for "men of the professor type" who might have a knack for codebreaking. By the time Harry Hinsley arrived in 1940, one of Denniston's early recruits had already become known around Bletchley Park for his striking eccentricities.

Alan Turing knew he was about to be attacked. Small particles, invisible to the naked eye, were about to be unleashed into the air he breathed. The effect, horrible. Coughing and sputtering, then watery and itchy eyes.

Turing did what was only logical—to his mind. For the rest of allergy season, whenever he rode his bike, he wore a gas mask to protect himself from hay fever.

He was an odd sight while on his bike, and not only because of his gas mask. His bike was broken, and rather than bother to repair it, he simply counted the number of rotations he had pedaled. He knew when his chain would stick, and immediately before that, he backpedaled the same number of rotations that he had pedaled forward. It was easy enough, and it saved him the trouble of fixing his bike. Plus, he never needed a bike lock. No one wanted to steal a broken bike.

(His lock found another purpose, however. Turing so prized his tea mug that he would chain it with the bike lock to the radiator in his office.)

Over and above his odd habits, what really stood out about Alan Turing was his genius.

Turing's intelligence was indisputable. One of his colleagues later remembered that "what you realize when you get to know a genius well is that there is all the difference between a very intelligent person and a genius. With very intelligent people . . . you say to yourself . . . I could have had that idea. You never had that feeling with Turing at all. He constantly surprised you with the originality of his thinking. It was marvelous."

Luckily for British codebreaking, other geniuses had come to Bletchley Park as well. About the same time Alan Turing began work with GC&CS, Denniston made another valuable recruit: Gordon Welchman.

In September 1938, Welchman was teaching mathematics—straight theory, not codebreaking—at Cambridge when he received Denniston's polite note asking whether he "would be willing to serve our country in the event of war."

Immediately, he said he would.

Welchman, a chess player with pink cheeks and wavy hair, which added up to "dashing good looks," one historian recounted, was nevertheless "a solemn old stick, without a great sense of humor," according to a friend.

But logic, not humor, was needed. When he began, "I was absolutely green," Welchman remembered, "and I simply tried to learn what I needed to know as quickly as possible."

For the rest of 1938 and the beginning of 1939, Turing and Welchman reported to GC&CS headquarters (which were in London at that time) for brief "short courses" on cryptology. Their names were often listed together with little check marks next to them, marking attendance for the professors just as they would have checked in their own students. And before long, they were helping expand Bletchley Park's fledgling group of codebreakers.

"For my part," Welchman remembered, "I quite shamelessly recruited friends and former students."

Stuart Milner-Barry was an old friend from Trinity College who "was not enjoying being a stockbroker," remembered Welchman. Milner-Barry, in turn, then recruited Hugh Alexander, a mathematician and a chess champion.

It wouldn't take long before Turing, Welchman, Alexander, and Milner-Barry earned the nickname of "the four wicked uncles of Bletchley Park." Some of the grandest discoveries and breakthroughs in European cryptography would come from their work.

But, for now, they still needed help.

Winter 1940—Paris, France

Alan Turing came to Paris for three days of talking and planning with the Polish cryptographers.

"We treated [Turing] as a younger colleague who had specialized in mathematical logic and was just starting out in cryptology," recalled Rejewski.

Turing had come to France to learn. He was only beginning to see how his skills with math could be used to break codes and ciphers; the Polish codebreakers had the experience and the insight he needed.

Then, on the last night Turing was in France, Rejewski, Zygalski, Różycki, Bertrand, Langer, and Turing went out to celebrate the successful visit. (In a certain cozy Parisian restaurant, they could talk freely about work: the waiters, chefs, and entire staff were employees of the Deuxième Bureau.)

The tables were decorated with long-petaled pink and purple flowers in small glass vases. Langer couldn't help showing off.

"Herbstzeitlose . . . Zimowity jesinne," he said, naming the flowers first in German and then in Polish.

Turing gazed on, blankly, until Jerzy Różycki spoke up. "*Colchicum autumnale*," he said, giving the flower's scientific name in Latin.

"Why, that's a powerful poison!" Turing cried, suddenly alert to the autumn crocuses on the table.

"It would suffice," Różycki said slowly, "to bite into and suck at a couple of stalks in order to attain eternity."

Langer had begun by boasting his talent with languages, but Turing and Różycki had revealed the danger beneath the petals. It was a reminder of the presence of death, never far from the codebreakers as the Nazi threat grew.

But the talk of suicide did not linger for long. Like so much else in the early 1940s, the visit balanced tenuously between levity and loss. The future was still too unknown for anything else.

Bletchley Park and PC Bruno needed a way to communicate across the English Channel. They couldn't keep meeting like this.

The answer lay in nearly four hundred miles of teletype cable laid between the two headquarters. Of course, this hard line was as vulnerable to being tapped as any. So, just like their enemy, the French and British codebreakers sent their messages using Enigma encryption.

The Germans were as much in the dark about breaking their own Enigma cipher as the Allies (the nations working together to defeat the Nazis). It would be just as difficult for the Germans to decipher a message without knowing the machine's settings and keys as it was for anyone else.

Still, the Bletchley Park and PC Bruno codebreakers used all of the little tricks they could to help make their messages as secure as possible. Longer messages were broken into several smaller transmissions, while shorter messages were padded with dummy letters to increase their length. This, the codebreakers hoped, would make it harder for an enemy to guess at a message's meaning.

The Nazis often used the same trick. The Germans liked to add an X to various places, both between words and between individual letters. They also added random phrases or words like *Gurkensalat* ["cucumber salad"] or *Schweinefleisch* ["pork"], just to throw off an enemy who might have a particular knack for guessing at presumed contents.

On the Allied side, one high-ranking French official who was responsible for sending Enigma transmissions to Bletchley Park went even further: he closed many messages with a phrase often used by the Germans to show loyalty to the Nazi cause, "Heil Hitler!"

Anything to confuse the enemy.

Anything to catch a weakness.

TWENTY

PHONY WAR

Fall 1939 through summer 1940—Europe

THE WAR—THE *REAL* war—was a long time coming.

Hitler had invaded Poland on September 1, 1939, and Britain and France had declared themselves to be Germany's enemies two days later.

And then . . . nothing.

Month after month, Hitler made no attempt to seize any more territory. The Allies did not try to take any of it back.

Each side deployed its navy. Each tried to blockade the other and limit their resources. There were small skirmishes and victories and death. But neither side rushed to any further action.

They watched. They waited. They made plans. They learned, uncovered, and deciphered all they could.

But the stalemate couldn't hold forever.

Who would move first, and when? And would the other side be ready?

TWENTY-ONE

A MISSING ROTOR

February 1940—off the coast of Scotland

SHALLOW WATER, MORE than any enemy, was death to a German U-boat. It was their nature and their design to dive.

"One of the first things you get through your head in submarines is that the deeper you get, the safer you are—hide and become invisible!" one U-boat sailor remembered.

U-boats traveled on the surface and carried a few guns, but their survival mechanism was escape. Dive, evade, survive, and rise again when strategy was on their side.

Which is why laying sea mines in the Firth of Clyde was nearly a suicide mission.

In February 1940, *U-33* under the command of Hans-Wilhelm von Dresky, a handsome thirty-two-year-old who was vain enough to care for his goatee even while deployed at sea, was sent to do just that. Traveling just five miles off the shore of Scotland, behind enemy lines in less than 130 feet of water—shallow enough that amateur scuba divers could nearly swim to its depths—they were assigned to lay mines. The shallow water left no place to hide.

It was strategic, to be sure. The Firth of Clyde was a narrow strip of water just west of Glasgow, which separated the Isle of

Arran from the rest of Scotland. British ships funneled into the narrow waterway would easily trigger the mines. It was an important place to disrupt the Royal Navy. Someone had to do it. Someone had to try.

In the weeks leading up to departure, the officers and crew of *U-33* were honored at celebrations and banquets. At one such feast, where the officers had been invited to sit at a top table with Nazi party leaders, one sailor forgot his manners and began ripping chicken meat from the bone, disregarding the utensils elegantly set before him. It was awkward until the most senior official there laughed, gave up his own utensils, and followed the man's example. There was no breach of etiquette or slip of manners that could not be put aside for the temporary comfort and ease of the men of *U-33*.

It was, after all, temporary. Mere days after the party, each sailor sealed his civilian clothes inside a tin box. It was easy storage, with only two outcomes: the men would retrieve the clothes when they arrived back safely or the very boxes they had just closed would be sent to their families as the only consolation for a fateful ending.

Dönitz himself, head of the U-boat fleet, came to see the men off. "Good luck, Hans," he shouted. "Look after yourself."

Dönitz had some reason to hope that Hans would in fact be able to look after himself and the forty-one other sailors aboard. *U-33* carried a torpedo; it wasn't a dedicated, defenseless ship built solely as a mine-laying vessel.

Which might be why Dönitz ignored the new rule that he himself had mandated. *U-33* was allowed to carry an Enigma machine.

There had been an earlier scare. In the first weeks of the war, *U-26* had gone to lay mines near Portland, England, and had not returned as anticipated. While the boat was unaccounted for, Dönitz worried not only for the safety of the crew but for the security of the Enigma onboard as well. *U-26* eventually turned up, but Dönitz had realized his weakness.

From then on, he ordered that no U-boat on a mine-laying mission—the most dangerous kind of mission—was allowed to carry an Enigma. He wrote in his war diary, "the consequent disadvantages and difficulties which will be experienced [due to not having an Enigma on board] . . . have to be accepted, as the risk of confidential books and cipher material falling into the enemy's hands, if the boat is lost in shallow water, is too great."

With *U-33*, Dönitz had ignored his own rule. The U-boat was carrying an Enigma.

It left port from Wilhelmshaven, Germany, on February 5, 1940. By the morning of Sunday, February 11, Dresky was in position off the coast of Scotland. As daylight approached, he sent his ship to the seafloor, escaping the sun and giving his men some peace from the surface swells that sent them bobbing and tossing sickeningly through the water. Only that night, with darkness masking their presence, did Dresky give the order for the U-boat to rise so they could begin their mission.

They worked quickly and quietly through the night. Nothing disturbed them until just before the dawn when a silhouette, dark against the dark horizon, came toward them. Outside on the bridge, Dresky and four lookouts watched silently as the other ship came closer and then passed by.

A few minutes later, the men stared in disbelief as the silhouette turned and began silently stalking toward them once more.

"Alarm!" Dresky shouted.

He jumped into the conning tower, flying down the ladder that connected the outside of the U-boat to the working belly within.

The other lookouts were close behind, and *U-33* launched into an emergency dive.

Down.

Down was the only escape.

Across the water on the British Royal Navy's HMS *Gleaner*, the hydrophone operator listened through the sea for telltale sounds of mechanical noise. He had been listening all night, searching for any sound that was more machine than animal. He hadn't heard anything until 2:50 A.M.

As the crew of *U-33* responded to Dresky's cry and threw the U-boat nose down to the depths, their engines came to life.

At that moment, the *Gleaner*'s hydrophone operator began hearing a rapid thrumming. Heavy *tonk-tonk-tonk* noises repeated twice each second. It was the exact acoustic signature of an engine. Quickly, he alerted the ship's officers.

On the *Gleaner*'s bridge, Lieutenant-Commander Hugh Price ordered his ship turned around one more time. In pursuit.

The *Gleaner* had not in fact seen *U-33* on its earlier pass. It was completing a routine patrol. It had not even seen—or heard—the U-boat until the moment the Germans had started to dive.

But now the chase was on.

Price ordered the *Gleaner*'s searchlights lit. As *U-33* pitched under the water, the British lookouts caught sight of a white line—spray issuing from the U-boat's periscope as it glided through and then slipped beneath the sea.

ASDIC, the early version of sonar developed by the British, was not subtle. Sound waves pulsed through the water and ricocheted off the metal sides of the U-boat. They called it "pinging," but the sound reverberated within the U-boat as if gravel had been dropped along the length of the U-boat's metal shell, making everyone inside tremble at the grating noise.

"He's got us," the U-boat's engineer said.

The *Gleaner* dropped its first depth charge at 3:53 A.M. These underwater bombs were specifically designed to destroy U-boats; the shock wave that was propelled through the water could be deadly, even if the bomb exploded away from the vessel.

It was the loudest noise anyone in *U-33* had ever heard. The explosion rocked the boat so violently that sailors in their beds were thrown onto the floor. The lights went out. Dim emergency bulbs gave scant view. Across the ship, instruments cracked, broken. Water started leaking in.

Dresky ordered the sailors into their escape suits—life jackets with small reservoirs of air for breathing—as the U-boat hit the seafloor. If their ship was wrecked underwater, it would be every man for himself as they tried to swim to the surface. At only 118

A WWII British minesweeper, the same type of ship as HMS Gleaner.
[Wikimedia Commons]

feet down, there was a chance the men, some of them, might survive. But at only 118 feet down, there was more of a chance that the depth charges would reach the U-boat first.

Over the next hour, the *Gleaner* dropped two more sets of depth charges. *U-33* couldn't stay on the seabed forever.

At 5:22 A.M., Dresky made the call.

"Surface! Air in all the tanks!" he shouted, deciding to surrender in order to save as many men as possible.

Water ballast, weighing down the U-boat and holding the ship captive at depth, exploded out of the tanks as air rushed in, and the now more-buoyant *U-33* began racing toward the surface.

"Abandon ship!" Dresky ordered. "Blow her up! Report by radio!"

Every man had his job. Some simply ran to the conning tower, flinging themselves up the ladder and jumping into the dark sea, moving themselves away as quickly as possible to let the rest of the sailors up and out. Others rushed to set fuses and open vents and hatches, preparing to scuttle their ship by blowing it to pieces rather than letting it—and all of the naval technology and secrets—fall prize to the enemy.

The fuses were timed so close to the order to abandon ship that *U-33*'s engineer was still climbing out of the conning tower when the wall of flame and pressure from the explosive charges threw him the rest of the way up and into the sea.

Dresky had climbed out immediately in front of the engineer, and the explosion tore his life jacket. In the water, waiting for the *Gleaner* to pick up survivors, Dresky led the men in giving three cheers for their destroyed vessel.

It was the last thing he ever did.

But not everyone's job was finished. Three of the men had been assigned to disassemble *U-33*'s Enigma. In the hectic minutes between the call to abandon ship and the explosions that would render the vessel useless, these three men were to take the Enigma's rotors, hide them in their pockets, and then dump them into the sea. That way, even if the enemy had somehow managed to stop the fuses or the explosion did not fully scuttle the ship, Enigma's secrets would be safe.

Two men completed their duties.

But on the deck of the *Gleaner*, having been rescued from freezing water and taken captive as a prisoner of war, Friedrich Kumpf turned to Heinz Rottmann, an officer.

"Herr Oberleutnant, I forgot to throw the wheels away."

Kumpf was sitting, covered in a blanket and huddled close to the other German men, each trying to warm their bodies, which had barely escaped hypothermia. Rottmann himself had fainted from the cold while waiting two hours for rescue. He only came to in a bathtub of warm water on the *Gleaner*.

Now, turning away from the young German sailor, Oberleutnant Rottmann went to Kumpf's pants, which were hanging up to dry.

They were empty.

A short distance away, a British sailor spoke with the *Gleaner*'s commander. The British sailor had searched the clothing of each German man, as he was supposed to do with prisoners. He didn't understand what he had found, but he handed it to his commander as instructed. In one of the pockets, drenched and dripping with seawater, he had found a metal piece that "looked like the gear-wheel off a bicycle."

TWENTY-TWO

DARK

Spring 1940—Bletchley Park, England

THE GERMAN NAVY was up to *eight* Enigma rotors.

Back in the early 1930s, when the Enigma cipher first began, there had been just three rotors. Rejewski had broken Enigma with that lineup. Then, before the invasion of Poland in 1939, the Germans had added two more rotors. That change had temporarily thwarted the Zygalski sheets and had permanently ended the bomba, Rejewski's mechanical invention to help break Enigma. Now, less than a year later, there were three more.

But Friedrich Kumpf had forgotten to empty his pockets, and now two of the new rotors were on their way to Bletchley Park.

By having the rotors in their hands, the codebreakers didn't need to mathematically solve for the wiring. They could physically trace the path of the circuits and understand the connections with absolute certainty.

Yet no one in Hut 8 celebrated.

Dönitz had made the naval Enigma net far more complicated than other nets. Understanding the rotors was only the first, small step.

To begin with, Dönitz had eliminated the repeated indicator

setting, the three letters that explained how to arrange the rotors; under Dönitz's order, the German navy only included a single set of the indicator settings in their preamble. Rejewski's bomba had relied on the indicator being typed twice. Dönitz's decision meant that the Polish bomba wouldn't work in Hut 8 at Bletchley Park. Never repeat something that you want kept secret.

Then there was the matter of codebooks.

With most Enigma nets, operators chose the three-letter indicator themselves. That, Dönitz decided, was a weakness as well.

Dönitz was concerned that his operators wouldn't choose truly random combinations of letters. Humans are lazy; we inevitably fall back to using patterns, and patterns weaken a cipher. So Dönitz had instructed his men to create codebooks written with pages and pages of three-letter combinations, which his operators could then use as indicators.

To make matters even more difficult for Bletchley Park, the naval Enigma operators then used *another* codebook to modify their chosen three-letter indicator, which added more confusion and made the final result even harder to decipher. Before any key was struck, the Enigma operator swapped pairs of letters using a bigram table.

It would look something like this:

EH=UO	XE=LV
TX=RF	UM=DH
YM=PW	JK=TR
LV=XE	EC=MU
RW=QA	EW=XM

And on and on, for every pair of letters possible.

Of course, there wasn't just one bigram table—there were nine. Dönitz was so concerned about security that he had his men create a full nine sets of tables instructing Enigma operators how to swap pairs of letters in the message indicator. The naval Enigma was a cipher within a cipher, with so many manipulations and modifications that each message was wound through mazes of hidden meanings.

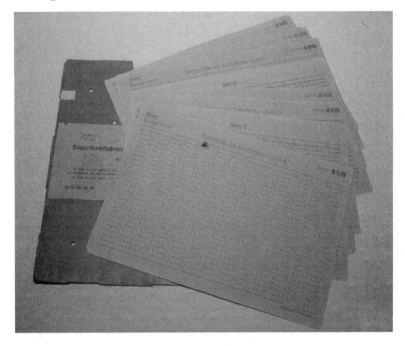

Bigram tables.
[www.cryptomuseum.com]

At Bletchley Park, the codebreakers were stuck. They understood the Enigma. They even had a grasp on the new rotors. But without a copy of the bigram tables, they would never read a single message.

"Further advance would depend on capturing more naval material—or at least on obtaining detailed information from knowledgeable prisoners of war," wrote Hinsley about the work on the naval Enigma in Hut 8.

Luckily, other Enigma nets were more easily broken.

John Herivel, a twenty-one-year-old mathematician who worked on the German army/air force net in Hut 6, was relaxing after work one night when he had a "happy brainwave."

The Enigma operators on the German army/air force net didn't have any codebooks, and they didn't use any bigram tables. They chose the indicator settings themselves.

What if, Herivel guessed, the operators on the German army/air force net didn't turn their rotors after positioning the ring setting? Suppose that a lazy operator used the same letters, or letters that were very close, for a ring setting *and* an indicator setting. If this was true, the codebreakers could solve for one setting and instantly know the other.

One morning in May, Herivel came in to work to see his colleagues clustered around his desk, reading German army/air force messages that had been broken using his idea. They called it the Herivel Tip.

"You won't be forgotten," Welchman promised the young man.

Another set of mistakes by the German army/air force Enigma operators, which was then exploited by the British codebreakers, began to be known as sillies or Cillies. It was a taunt created from the literal pronunciation of the first three-letter message setting that was found this way: CIL.

Like the discovery of the Herivel Tip, the Cillies worked because the Enigma operators weren't careful. They were *supposed* to choose a random set of three letters for the indicator setting; patterns, instead, were easier for an operator to think of.

The Enigma keyboard looked like this:

QWERTZUIO

ASDFGHJK

PYXCVBNML

If an operator set his first message key to QAY and his second to WSX—both sequences that go nearly straight down the keyboard from the first line to the second to the third—then the cryptologists had an easy guess that his next setting would be EDC. The Cillies were keyboard patterns like this, and they made for easy guessing by the codebreakers.

"Unbelievable!" Welchman later wrote. "Yet it actually happened, and it went on happening. . . . Indeed . . . it seems to me that we must have been entirely dependent on Herivel Tips and Cillies from the invasion of France to the end of the Battle of Britain."

In Hut 6, intelligence started flowing from messages that the cryptographers deciphered and handed over to translators and analysts in Hut 3.

But in Hut 8, the cryptographers working on the German naval Enigma net had no such luck. Dönitz had taken great care to ensure that the Herivel Tip and Cillies, two "astonishingly bad habits," as Welchman wrote, would never occur during operation of the naval Enigma.

Hut 8 was completely dark.

The single bright spot in their efforts to decrypt the naval Enigma came not from the content of the messages but from looking at all of the parts of the messages *except* the meaning of the text.

Traffic analysis examined elements such as the location of message transmission, message frequency, operator frequency (who was sending messages and how often each individual sent them), and even if messages were repeated on different radio frequencies. It was an art, not a science, which "called more for immersion in detail than for experience at sea," Hinsley wrote. But by May 1940, Hinsley had become a master.

That month, Hinsley noticed something weird. Messages intended for ships in the Baltic Sea were sent once and then exactly repeated on other frequencies.

Never repeat something that you want kept secret.

Like everything else at Bletchley Park, Hinsley pieced his insight together through part intuition and part lucky guess: Germany was about to invade Norway. Their ships from the Baltic Sea were moving north.

The most difficult part of the whole problem, Hinsley quickly realized, was getting anyone in England to believe him. The naval Enigma hadn't produced any useful intelligence so far, and the Admiralty wasn't used to getting phone calls from codebreakers at Bletchley Park.

"In keeping with the scarcity of intelligence, communication with the Admiralty was distinctly primitive," Hinsley wrote. "I used a direct telephone line which I had to activate by turning a handle energetically before speaking."

When he was finally connected with someone, "they showed little interest in what I said."

He was young, not even graduated from college, and had never sailed on a single navy vessel. Why would admirals pay attention to him?

But in June, two German battle cruisers, the *Scharnhorst* and the *Gneisenau*, sank the British aircraft carrier HMS *Glorious* and her two destroyer escorts, HMS *Ardent* and HMS *Acasta*, off the coast of Norway. More than fifteen hundred men died in the freezing Atlantic water. Had the British admirals listened to Hinsley, those lives could've been saved.

The Royal Navy vowed to never make that mistake again.

"I was and I remain . . . full of admiration for the alacrity with which the [naval intelligence] responded to the loss of *Glorious*," Hinsley wrote.

The Admiralty quickly invited Hinsley to the British naval base at Scapa Flow, Scotland. From then on, the Admiralty "did all in its power to ensure through the regular exchange of visits . . . that there should be complete collaboration between the OIC [Operational Intelligence Center] and the Naval Section at Bletchley."

Hinsley and his method of traffic analysis—examining the location, frequency, and timing of messages—began to gain traction.

Even still, there was only so much that limited information could tell. The real story was inside the messages.

And the codebreakers still couldn't find a way in.

TWENTY-THREE

CERTAIN MECHANICAL DEVICES

Winter 1940—Letchworth, England

NO ONE IN the world had ever built a computer before. Few people had spent much time even thinking about the idea.

But Alan Turing was one of those people. And nearby, in Letchworth, the British Tabulating Machine Company made some calculators, which was just about as close as anyone had gotten to manufacturing computer parts.

Only a few years before the war, Turing had come up with the idea of a machine that could read a sequence of symbols, manipulate them according to a given but changeable set of instructions, and then write the answer out in another set of symbols. In this idea, he had just laid the foundations of all digital computers. (He not-so-humbly named the proposed machine after himself, calling it a Universal Turing Machine.)

As soon as he confronted the naval Enigma problem, Turing realized that a similar kind of machine would be needed to break the cipher. It would not need to reach quite the complexity of a Universal Turing Machine; it would need to do only one thing, decipher Enigma messages. But there was perhaps no one else more perfectly suited to think about how to mechanically break the German code than Alan Turing.

Turing arrived at Bletchley Park in the summer of 1939. By the advent of winter, he had a plan.

At the British Tabulating Machine Company, it fell to Harold Keen—nicknamed Doc because he used to carry around a big black bag like a doctor—to transform Turing's plans into reality.

"The engineers had their engineering skill, we had none of that," remembered Oliver Lawn, a young codebreaker sent to help translate Turing's instructions into plans that could be manufactured and assembled.

In five weeks, a fantastically quick timeline, possible only due to the war, the British Tabulating Machine Company had finished. Turing's bombe, named in honor of the Polish bomba, was ready.

Winter 1940—PC Bruno, outside Paris, France

The winter was as pleasant as it could be, all things considered, for the Polish codebreakers. They had ciphers to keep them busy during the day and managed to find ways to distract themselves—from war, from missing their families, from loneliness and homesickness—at night.

For all of their displacement and trauma, the Polish codebreakers fought to keep a positive attitude. But the same could not be said about their French host, especially regarding his feelings toward Bletchley Park.

"Bertrand's attitude toward the English was very French," Langer remembered. "He was most displeased with the fact that in 1939 the English were simply handed over the machine and the technique of breaking the codes, whereas he had spent a long time trying to obtain the machine."

Bertrand's anger was misplaced. It was Langer, not the codebreakers at Bletchley Park, who had kept Bertrand from Enigma.

But it was easier for Bertrand to be upset with someone far away. After all, Bertrand had his prize in the end: the talented Polish cryptographers were in France, working with his team.

And Bertrand was not about to let the Polish codebreakers, his prized guests, go free.

Denniston asked for them to come to England. Repeatedly. He even wrote to Stewart Menzies, the head of MI6, in the winter of 1940:

Dear Menzies,

Here are the names of the three young Poles, Jerzy Rozycki, Marian Rejewoli [sic], Henryk Zygalski. . . . The experience of these men may shorten our task by months. We possess certain mechanical devices which cannot be transferred to France. These young men possess ten years' experience and a short visit from them might prove of very great value.

Yours ever sincerely, A. G. Denniston

Bertrand was unmoved. Even with a request from Stewart Menzies, he would not let the Polish codebreakers leave. Denniston would just have to work through him. It was a handy way for an intelligence office to control information. By keeping Rejewski, Zygalski, and Różycki with him, Bertrand would know whatever the cryptographers knew. Intelligence was the most valuable currency.

"I am resigned to not having [the codebreakers] with us," Denniston finally wrote to Bertrand in February 1940. "You have said frankly that it is impossible, so I accept it."

Yet Bertrand could not have it all. Denniston had written correctly: "certain mechanical devices" were coming to Bletchley Park, and these would never leave the security of England.

February 1940—Bletchley Park, England

A single truck, weighed down with more than one ton of copper and steel, rumbled up the country road toward Bletchley Park. The machine in the trailer contained more than ten miles of wires and one million soldered connections woven into a nest of electrical relays between one hundred yellow, green, red, brown, and orange rotating cylinders. The massive machine measured an impressive eight feet tall, twelve feet wide, and three feet deep.

Bletchley Park bombe.
[Wikimedia Commons]

They had debated whether to have an escort, surrounding the truck with a caravan of police and armored cars. In the end, though, it was decided that the safest course of action was to draw as little attention to it, and to Bletchley Park, as possible.

Alan Turing's first bombe arrived in the back of an open, flatbed trailer without any other accompanying vehicles or fanfare.

Rejewski's bomba had worked because the Germans repeated themselves: the indicator setting was typed twice at the beginning of each message. Turing's bombe bet on a different strategy. He guessed that, at some point, the codebreakers would figure out at least part of an Enigma message.

Guessing was a trick as old as cryptography itself. Humans were predictable.

Turing bet that parts of naval Enigma messages would be predictable, too. Certainly, loyal officers would not stop signing off "Heil Hitler!" And regular reports might very well devolve into a repetitive pattern. Patterns were vulnerabilities. Never repeat something you want kept secret.

Turing's bombe was built around the assumption that the codebreakers would soon be able to match a section of plaintext messages with their ciphertext equivalent. Like something that students "used for cheating in an examination," Welchman wrote, the codebreakers called these hoped-for pairs of plaintext and ciphertext letters "cribs." After the codebreakers discovered a crib, they could then arrange certain letters and create a "menu" as a starting point for Turing's bombe.

That, at least, was the idea.

Victory, the first bombe at Bletchley Park, was installed on March 1, 1940. It was like "some Eastern goddess who was destined to become the oracle of Bletchley," wrote secret service officer Frederick Winterbotham.

But for all its prophesying potential, the oracle stayed silent. It needed a crib. Without it, Victory was just a mess of metal and wires, useful to no one. Until then, all the bombe could do was gather dust, waiting for a crib that might never come.

TWENTY-FOUR

NEARLY DROWNED

April 1940—Wilhelmshaven, Germany

"NINTH APRIL. THICK fog. No wind," German boatswain Karl Reitz recorded in his diary. It was perfect weather for deception.

Schiff 26 was a German fishing boat, now heavily armed and fully converted to a military ship. Torpedoes, explosives, depth charges, and mines filled her storage areas and spilled over into high piles on her deck. It was all bound for the German forces eagerly waiting armament in Norway.

But stealth, not firepower and brawn, was called for on the journey there.

By late April, everything was ready. The sailors had draped canvas boat covers over the huge stern gun, disguising it as a lifeboat, and had hidden ammunition stacked on deck under fishing nets and baskets. Wooden covers were thrown over the two torpedo tubes sticking out of the foredeck. The Germans changed out of their uniforms and went unwashed, pretending to be unkempt civilians as they hoisted a Dutch flag. As a final touch, they stenciled a fake Dutch name on the sides of the vessel: *Polares*.

Just before they left Wilhelmshaven, the crew of *Schiff 26/Polares* watched as another German ship came back into port and listened as those sailors described the harrowing story of rescuing survivors: the screams of drowning men, unable to reach help, and then the ship's decks filled with corpses.

"Terrible sight. The crew were unable to eat for some time, it affected them so much," Karl Reitz wrote.

Reitz and the rest of the crew could only hope that their disguises kept them safe.

But they weren't the first to attempt to cloak a military ship as a common fishing boat. The British navy had already been warned.

April 1940—off the coast of Norway

At 10:30 A.M. on April 26, 1940, lookouts on the British destroyer HMS *Griffin* spotted a small, apparently civilian, ship.

Commander John Lee-Barber knew the story: reports had already mentioned that another ordinary and non-military-looking ship had launched torpedoes at an unsuspecting British vessel. Deceit, the British were quickly learning, was a favorite tool of the German navy.

Lee-Barber hadn't been fired upon—yet—and he wanted to keep it that way.

He ordered the *Griffin* turned from its course, heading to cut off the smaller boat.

On *Schiff 26/Polares*, Oberleutnant Heinz Engelein was outgunned and outmaneuvered. Even with all of the extra armament and ammunition he was carrying, his boat was no match for the British destroyer. He was beat.

Engelein had orders to scuttle the ship if it looked like it would be captured. Charges had already been laid, just in case. With all of the explosives it was carrying, the ship would easily be destroyed. The blast from the ammunition would kill anyone close; the heavy seas would take many more.

Engelein couldn't condemn his men to death. So he ignored orders. He prepared to be boarded by the British.

Schiff 26/Polares's Enigma machine went over the side, sinking under its own weight in the wild, frantic seas.

Quickly, Engelein stuffed codebooks and papers into duffel bags, knowing that this information was almost as precious as the machine itself.

One duffel bag he weighted down with ammunition. It immediately slipped beneath the water, never to return to the surface again.

The other bag, however, was thrown overboard with its own weight as the only ballast.

In the midst of waves and wind, it floated.

From high on the deck of the *Griffin*, Gunner "Florrie" Foord caught sight of a small bag floating in the water. He threw himself overboard, pausing only long enough to quickly tie a line around his waist.

In the heaving seas, swells rising and dropping back, he caught hold of the bag. Clasping it tightly, Foord felt a yank as his crewmates began to haul him and the bag up onto the deck.

Then the line snapped.

Foord fell into the water, disappearing under the waves. The long, horrible moment stretched on, as sailors on the *Griffin* stared down at the water, straining to see him once more.

And then, still managing to clutch the bag to his chest, Foord bobbed up again.

The sailors threw down a second line, but it slipped through Foord's one-armed grasp. He would not let the bag go.

Finally, on the third try, they sent a line with a loop, and Foord managed to squeeze his shoulders through the lasso. They hauled him onto the deck, freezing cold and close to drowning, still holding the canvas bag.

Two days later, Commander Lee-Barber sailed back into a British harbor with *Schiff 26/Polares* in tow. He immediately handed over the bag that Foord had rescued from the sea.

TWENTY-FIVE

BOMBES AND SPIDER BOMBES

May 1940—Bletchley Park, England

OBERLEUTNANT HEINZ ENGELEIN had cleared *Schiff 26/Polares* of any piece of paper with Enigma information. He had done an immaculate job.

Which meant that Gunner Foord from the *Griffin* had rescued treasure. There, inside the bag, the cryptographers found plaintext messages written exactly alongside their ciphered versions.

They were perfect cribs.

And that wasn't the only prize. At Bletchley Park, the codebreakers spent days weeding through the different papers, translating and analyzing as they went. One small bit of loose paper was overlooked at first, but, when they did finally examine it, the British codebreakers discovered a complete list of settings for the plugboard, telling the operators which pairs of letters to connect on which days.

It was "an interesting example of the importance of retaining the most insignificant scraps for expert examination," remembered Hugh Alexander.

Between the crib and the plugboard settings, Alan Turing had enough to create a menu and set his bombe to work.

Victory whirred to life. "Like a battery of knitting needles,"

Welchman wrote, the drums stepped around and around. Clicks, like the cadence of soldiers marching to battle, echoed across the room every time the drums rotated into new positions.

Then, with a shudder, the bombe stopped, and a great space of silence followed.

The codebreakers read off the settings and rushed to a checking machine, a replica of an Enigma machine that was designed to test Victory's results.

But the settings didn't work.

When the cryptologists set up the checking machine as the bombe instructed and typed in the ciphertext message, the translated results certainly weren't words that meant anything in German.

So the codebreakers went back to the bombe and started it up again.

It took weeks. Whenever the bombe reached what it thought could be a solution, it would seize and jolt to a stop. Operators would rush to the dials and note settings, and the codebreakers would test what the bombe suggested. Over and over, the process ran continuously day and night.

Eventually, it did work.

At last, after almost a month of starting, stopping, checking, failing, and trying again, one of the bombe's solutions translated the gibberish of Enigma ciphertext into a plain, readable German message.

It was the first time the naval Enigma had been read during the war.

But it was hardly victory.

By the time the bombe produced usable results, the information contained in the decrypted Enigma messages was nearly two months old. The cryptologists would never be able to influence the war at that pace.

To make matters even worse, not every crib would work on Turing's bombe. Victory needed a menu composed of "loops," letters that referenced other letters and continued until the first letters were referenced once again.

Cribs—even weak ones—were hard to come by. Asking for cribs that followed specific rules seemed like one prayer too many to be answered.

While they waited for the next opportunity, an idea "flashed into my mind," remembered Gordon Welchman.

"When this new method . . . came to me, I couldn't believe it," he wrote. "But I sat down with a few colored pencils, drew a simple wiring diagram, and convinced myself the idea could work."

He hurried over and showed Turing. "Turing was incredulous at first, as I had been, but when he had studied my diagram he . . . became as excited about it as I was."

In Letchworth, at the British Tabulating Machine Company, Doc Keen agreed. He could create Welchman's circuits with a simple square lattice, a grid of twenty-six by twenty-six electrical terminals called a "diagonal board." Nearly two extra miles of twisted wires connecting the new circuits and relays; they named the new machines spider bombes.

By midsummer 1940, Doc Keen had the first prototype ready. An eighteen-year-old new recruit to Bletchley Park, Richard Pendered, was sent to the factory in Letchworth see if the spider bombe would work.

He chose a hard crib without any of the explicit loops that Turing's original bombe would have needed. It was such a difficult starting point that no one knew if the spider bombe could actually solve the settings.

They switched it on. Sparks literally began to fly.

The bombe churned away, relays clicking open and closed. Factory workers ran up and down the array, constantly checking connections. Every time a wire came loose, the whole process came to a halt. Whatever needed to be tightened or replaced was fixed, and they started the spider bombe up once again.

Pendered held his breath.

Then the machine stopped once more. Nothing was loose. Nothing had come apart.

The spider bombe had found a solution—or, it thought it had.

Operators dashed up again, hand cranking the wheels back to read each position. Pendered took the list of settings to the opposite side of the factory. A checking machine, just like the ones at Bletchley Park, was ready to test the results.

To the astonishment of everyone watching, Pendered was able to arrange the rotors, rings, and plugboard just as the spider bombe suggested. It had given him something reasonable to try using a crib that would have failed in Turing's original bombe. It was a huge success on only the first run.

But when Pendered typed in the next part of the ciphertext, the letters that came out of the checking machine still didn't form German words. The spider bombe was more capable than Victory, but it still might take weeks to get to the *right* answer with such a complicated crib.

Day after day, Pendered walked back and forth between the spider bombe and the checking machine, each time trying the new array of settings the spider bombe suggested.

Until finally, when he sat down at the checking machine, the Enigma lit up in order:

W-I-R-H-O-F-F-E-N.

Pendered translated the German to English:

"We hope."

The spider bombe had found the correct settings, and the hopes of Bletchley Park flew high once more.

The codebreakers still needed cribs—and they didn't have any more of those. They still needed the bigram tables—and they didn't have those, either.

But when they did get the messages and codebooks, Bletchley Park would be ready.

TWENTY-SIX

HUNTING AT NIGHT

Fall 1940—Atlantic Ocean

"ONE OF OUR most natural instincts is the desire, if fight we must, to be as strong as possible, not to be left to fight alone, but to seek the help of others," wrote Dönitz.

The only way for Germany to defeat Britain was to starve her people and industry into surrender, and that meant a blockade of the island nation. While the Germans seized land on the European continent with their army and their air force, Dönitz and his U-boats went to work in the sea. In the middle of the Atlantic, out of easy reach of land-based planes, they attacked.

Allied merchant ships soon started traveling in convoys, where armed ships guarded cargo and passenger vessels. But the weapons were makeshift, with the Allies converting old fishing boats into armored militias, just as the Germans were. The convoys were vulnerable, if the Germans could just get the strategy right.

There was strength in numbers.

One U-boat alone could not take down a British supply convoy. One U-boat alone was weak.

So the U-boats began attacking together.

At the beginning of a patrol, they spread out, sailing alone and spying on as much of the Atlantic as possible.

Convoy of Allied ships traveling together for safety.
[Wikimedia Commons]

Until one spotted an enemy.

Over Enigma-enciphered radio transmissions, the first U-boat alerted the others. Then it sank down and waited, hidden far below the surface, biding its time until a group formed. Finally, when they had gathered and surrounded their prey, they attacked and devoured.

Observe. Identify. Gather. Assault.

The Germans called it a wolfpack.

In July 1940, the month before Dönitz let his wolfpacks loose in the Atlantic, the entire U-boat fleet sank just thirty-eight ships. In September, the month after wolfpacks began, they sank fifty-nine ships, and in October they sank sixty-three. It was the most ships sunk in a single month since the start of the war, and the numbers only went up from there.

Leading up to the war, Dönitz had practiced wolfpack maneuvers with the full navy several times. Thousands of sailors and officers knew about the tactics. Dönitz was convinced "that it would be quite impossible to keep these new tactics a secret."

Yet, somehow, "the change [in strategy] caught us unawares," remembered British naval captain Stephen Roskill. "The enemy had adopted a form of attack which we had not foreseen and against which neither tactical nor technical countermeasures had been prepared."

The British navy had ASDIC, their early sonar device. With this, they thought they had the means of conquering the U-boat threat. "The U-boat will never again be capable of confronting us with the problem with which we found ourselves faced in 1917 [the First World War]," according to an official Admiralty communication in 1937.

They were wrong.

It is difficult, Dönitz countered, "for a naval officer who has been educated and trained for surface warfare clearly to appreciate and assimilate the importance of any other type of fighting, such as submarine warfare."

At Bletchley Park, the codebreakers sat in front of stacks of U-boat transmissions, signals that an enemy ship had been found and that they were gathering the wolfpack to attack. It was easy enough for the British and Allied stations to intercept the transmission, but it was impossible to read any early warning contained within the message.

To the hapless codebreakers at Bletchley Park, the growing pile of ciphertext spelled only doom.

TWENTY-SEVEN

JOAN

Fall 1940—Bletchley Park, England

JOAN CLARKE HAD the fifth desk in Hut 8.

They had put her, at first, in the "big room" with the other women—the typists, the machine operators, the secretaries—but that was a mistake. She had been recruited by Welchman himself, and she had completed an advanced mathematics degree at Cambridge, like the rest of the team. She should have been in Hut 8 from the start. But codebreaking—and mathematics—was seen as a man's field; they hadn't been expecting a woman.

Physically moving from the big room to Hut 8 was fairly easy. Arranging Clarke's position was an entirely different question. They had to invent a job for her, since codebreakers were clearly "men of the professor type," and she didn't fit that description. They called her a "linguist," but that was a lie. When asked to fill out forms stating which languages she had fluency in, Clarke bluntly stated, "languages: none." Clarke was a mathematician and a codebreaker; her gender mattered only to Bletchley Park administration, not to her or her peers.

When they eventually wanted to promote her, the head of GC&CS approached her to say that they might have to enroll her in the Women's Royal Naval Service (the Wrens) just so that she would be adequately paid. They didn't have a way to promote a woman as a codebreaker. It wasn't a joke, and though Clarke laughed it off, the sting of it must have been very real.

Clarke had the skills to get the job done, which was all that mattered to her and the rest of the team in Hut 8. Because, while they waited for another crib, there was still plenty of work to do.

Turing, called "the Prof" by everyone at Bletchley Park, was developing another, as yet unproven, technique: Banburismus, which examined the number of times letters were repeated in messages. This new method would never break Enigma on its own, but it could help the spider bombe. If—*when*—another crib was discovered, Banburismus would cut down on the time needed to solve for Enigma settings by giving the bombe as much information as possible.

That is, like everything else, if it worked.

Clarke got right to it, determined to prove Turing's theory could help in practice.

It became a game. Banburismus was "enjoyable, not easy enough to be trivial, but not difficult enough to cause a nervous breakdown," Hugh Alexander, working with Clarke in Hut 8, remembered. And Clarke was good at it.

It "was often so enthralling," Clarke wrote, "that the analyst due to go home at the end of the shift would be unwilling to hand over the workings."

Bletchley Park was staffed around the clock. They traded off the night shifts, taking turns for a week at a time. Clarke remembered that one of the men "lent me his alarm clock so that I could relieve him at 2 A.M."

By November, Clarke's work with Banburismus, the spider bombe, and a few good guesses at cribs from *Schiff 26/Polares* had put together a miracle: three more days of messages had been broken. Bletchley Park could now read any naval Enigma message sent on April 14, May 8, and June 26.

What they found brought them up cold.

Enigma wasn't a break-once-and-understand-forever cipher. Settings changed every day. The rotors were swapped and rearranged. The plugboard connections were altered. Even something as foundational as the bigram tables could be rewritten.

And they were.

Among the messages from June 26, several told a chilling story: new bigram tables had been introduced on July 1.

The pieces of tables that Turing had managed to weave together were now useless scrap. The German navy was using an entirely different set of codebooks.

"The prospect of reading the naval Enigma," Clarke said rather bluntly, wholly "depended on another capture."

Not only did the codebreakers need cribs, they needed a whole new set of bigram tables, too.

Bletchley Park was in the dark, and the German wolfpack hunted best at night.

TWENTY-EIGHT

OPERATION RUTHLESS

September 12, 1940—Admiralty, London, England

REAR ADMIRAL JOHN GODFREY was the British director of naval intelligence. It was time, he decided, for his department to think up "cunning schemes" to "pinch" some codebooks. His assistant—none other than Ian Fleming, who would one day create the character and stories of James Bond—was ready.

Fleming handed him a proposal.

OPERATION RUTHLESS

- Obtain from Air Ministry an air-worthy German bomber.
- Pick a tough crew of five, including a pilot, W/T [wireless telegraph] operator and word-perfect German speaker. Dress them in German Air Force uniform, add blood and bandages to suit.
- Crash plane in the Channel after making S.O.S. to rescue service in P/L [plain language].
- Once aboard [German] rescue boat, shoot German crew, dump overboard, bring rescue boat back to English port.

Godfrey approved it immediately.

Mere days later, Fleming flew down to Dover, fully set to be the "word-perfect German speaker" on the crew, but he was quickly cut from the roster. Fleming knew all about the Enigma operation at Bletchley Park; if the Germans caught him, the secret might get out. It was too risky to let him be a part of the action.

In Dover, Group Captain H. J. Wilson had restored a captured German bomber, a Heinkel He 111. It was Wilson who pointed out that crash-landing the plane in the Channel, in seas that were bound to be choppy and dangerous in the fall weather, would undoubtedly crumple the plane's nose, immediately sink the aircraft, and almost certainly injure the crew. These wet, cold, and likely battered crewmen were then supposed to overwhelm, disarm, and dispose of the Germans who rescued them. It was a long shot at best.

German Heinkel He 111, the type Ian Fleming
proposed crashing in Operation Ruthless.
[Wikimedia Commons]

When Wilson was asked point-blank if he would fly in Operation Ruthless, he declined, none too politely. He declared that he "preferred to work on successful operations than to win a posthumous Victoria Cross." Instead of finding the best men for the team, Fleming and the other officers changed tactics to begin recruiting for a suicide mission. The pilot who finally volunteered was lovesick and depressed.

However, even after giving his blunt opinion about their chances of success, Wilson did what he could to help. He strengthened the plane's nose, reinforcing it as much as possible to withstand the forces of the planned crash. And he invented a way of injecting oil into the plane's exhaust to make it look like the engine was on fire, all the better for deceiving their German audience.

In the end, it didn't matter. On the appointed nights when the mission was to take place, the British men did not spot a single German ship. Two reconnaissance planes flew over the water, and neither saw anything. Radio intelligence on the ground couldn't find any trace of German ships close by in the Channel, either. It was pointless to risk the attempt if no Germans would respond.

The vice admiral at Dover wrote to Godfrey, "Possibly Portsmouth area may be more fruitful."

But they had no more luck in Portsmouth than they did in Dover. Eventually, the plan was abandoned. They'd just have to steal the codebooks another way.

Back at Bletchley Park, Turing was furious. Four days after Operation Ruthless was called off, he and a colleague marched into the GC&CS administrative office "like undertakers cheated of a nice corpse . . . all in a stew about the cancellation of Operation Ruthless."

Turing was *so* close. After designing the bombe and adding Welchman's improvements. After developing techniques like Banburismus to speed up the bombes. They had many, many ways of breaking the code. But every method depended on knowing the bigram tables.

Yet even Turing knew that the Germans might very well change their tables again. The first pinch would likely not be the last.

TWENTY-NINE

DOUBT

May 31, 1940—North Sea, off the coast of Lowestoft, England

THE OUTLINE OF the British anti-submarine ship loomed over the commander of *U-13* as soon as he opened the conning tower hatch. It had been a stressful night, with depth charges exploding around the Germans as the British ship hunted the U-boat. By 2 A.M., the German commander knew the game was over.

"Everybody out!" he shouted, and the twenty-three-man crew plunged into the water.

As his shipmates abandoned the vessel, Chief Engineer Grandjean ran through the ship, opening vent after vent, intent on sinking the U-boat before the enemy could reach it. Suddenly, as he opened the final vents, the bow of the ship sliced between the waves and furiously shot down, disappearing beneath the surface.

The hatch slammed shut as the U-boat hurled to the depths with Grandjean—the last man aboard—still inside. Wrapping one arm around the conning tower ladder, he forced opened the hatch with his other hand. Grandjean struggled to keep hold of the ladder's rungs, pushing desperately through the wall of water to make his escape. Finally out of the U-boat, he attempted at first to slow his progress up to the surface, allowing time for his body to adjust to the changing pressure. But after a few moments, Grandjean panicked and swam as fast as he could.

Half an hour later, he was picked up by a passing ship. Somehow, everyone from *U-13* had survived.

The U-boat was wrecked, but the British navy still salvaged what they could.

To the German officers back in Berlin, the question was, what had they found?

U-13 had carried an Enigma machine. Which meant it had also held Enigma codebooks. Had either been seized?

Grandjean had opened the vents; he had flooded *U-13* as ordered. That, more than fully scuttling the ship, was important to keeping Enigma's secret. Every Enigma codebook was printed with red ink on pink paper. It made them easy to spot, but its true purpose was much more powerful: the ink and paper were both designed to dissolve upon contact with water. Flooding the U-boat should have easily destroyed the codes.

But clearly the crew had been captured. Clearly the U-boat was no longer in German control.

It was enough to make Dönitz nervous. One week after the capture of *U-13*, he questioned the naval communications service. Had the Enigma cipher been compromised? Should they alter Enigma procedures?

The answer came back: carry on without changes.

Twelve days later, Dönitz, unsatisfied, asked again. Was the Enigma secure?

The naval communications service explained once more that several settings and the bigram tables, which Grandjean's flooding had likely destroyed, were protecting the device. To jeopardize Enigma, the enemy would have to have access to all of these.

"The existence of any of these conditions and especially the existence of all of them at the same time is most unlikely," the naval communications service soothed its commander once again.

Dönitz let himself be reassured.

THIRTY

ASCHÉ

March 10, 1940—Lugano, Switzerland

EVEN AFTER THE invasion of Poland, Hans-Thilo Schmidt, code named Asché, had continued to pass information to his French handlers. But as the months wore on, there was a growing threat of discovery to France's most valuable asset. Until finally, in early March 1940, Schmidt met with a French agent named Henri Navarre near the Swiss-Italian border.

"It was sunny," Navarre reported a few days later, "the view of the lake and the snow-covered Alps was impressive. While taking a stroll in the sun, we went to lunch on the Riva Paradiso. [Schmidt] had reserved a table set a little apart from the others on the terrace of a luxury restaurant. We were able to chat without any fear of being overheard."

Schmidt, as always, had important news to report: his brother had been promoted once again. As the head of the 39th Panzer Corps, his brother had been invited to meet with Hitler himself. Over lunch, not even a month prior, the Führer had presented plans for Fall Gelb[Operation Yellow]: the invasion of western Europe.

Schmidt's information lined up with what other intelligence networks had pieced together. The Germans were coming for France.

There was something else, though. Schmidt seemed more upset than ever before. He had often passed on difficult information, but this time, Navarre became concerned.

"I observed that he seemed worried," Navarre remembered. "I asked if something was distressing him."

"I hope Monsieur Barsac [Bertrand] and Monsieur Lemoine have given nothing to the Poles that could implicate me," Schmidt replied.

If there had been anything left behind at the Polish cipher office, or at the Gale outside of Warsaw, it was all in Nazi hands now.

"I advised him that if he really felt in danger that he should flee to France," Navarre remembered.

"I'd rather die!" cried Schmidt. "It would jeopardize my family and especially my brother. I will never do that."

But he realized that it was too dangerous to keep passing secrets. This would be his last meeting with the Deuxième Bureau.

"He shook my hand for a long time," said Navarre, "asking me to send his best wishes to . . . Barsac . . . and Lemoine."

"I so wanted to avoid war and save my country from the disaster that is at its door!" said the impassioned Schmidt.

He had provided intelligence to the Deuxième Bureau for almost nine years. Though his first motivations might have been money, in the end, he wanted the same as everyone else: peace.

THIRTY-ONE

OPERATION PAULA

May 1940—France

"SOLDIERS OF THE western front! The hour of decisive combat has arrived. . . . The struggle that begins today will settle the fate of the nation for a thousand years." Nine months after the Germans invaded Poland, Hitler commanded his forces forward once more. The Phony War was over.

It began in the European Low Countries, just as Schmidt had warned: Belgium, Netherlands, and Luxembourg. The German military invaded and cut across the countryside, surrounding and trapping British and French troops against the English Channel. Newly elected British prime minister Winston Churchill ordered the evacuation of more than three hundred thousand Allied soldiers from Dunkirk, France.

Luxembourg surrendered. The Netherlands surrendered. Belgium surrendered. But they were only a prelude, a means to an end. The real goal was France.

PC Bruno, at Château de Vignolles, was directly in the line of the attack. The French codebreakers were evacuated to Paris within days of the start of the German offensive.

The Deuxième Bureau headquarters at 2 bis Avenue de Tourville were disappointing compared to the Saxon Palace and Château de Vignolles. It was a "long, drab building," recounted one historian, and after a few days spent in a secured hotel, the Polish cryptographers found themselves not only working at, but living as well at the headquarters.

Even that wouldn't last for long.

Like their British counterparts in Hut 6, Rejewski, Zygalski, and Różycki could decrypt Enigma messages from the German army and air force. In late May, they read, in detail, what was coming. One translated Luftwaffe (German air force) message was explicit:

> *While conducting Paula the squadron including infantry (3 fight groups) flies over Sankt Marie for 1500 meters, older planes 10 minutes ahead. True take on time will follow from delivery. Flight course south of Reims. Target approach (targets are Corbeil, Melun, Nangis). After the strike, turn south and return flight over Sedan.*

When one German unit couldn't quite figure out what "Paula" stood for, the Polish codebreakers read in some disbelief the explicit definition: "Paula = Paris."

Hitler was coming for the heart of France.

The Allies knew the German plans, yet no one mounted a defense of the city. The French forces were spread thin; there wasn't anyone to come to Paris's rescue. Bertrand later wrote that the commander in chief of the French air force's hands were tied: "he did not have the hundred fighter aircraft necessary unless he stripped the front of that number." And the aircraft at the front, perilously trying to hold back the Nazi push into France, could not be moved.

On May 15, the French prime minister, Paul Reynaud, called British prime minister Winston Churchill in despair. "We have been defeated. We are beaten. We have lost the battle. The road to Paris is open."

Churchill immediately left for France and was in Paris the next day. Confronting Reynaud, he demanded, "Where are the strategic reserves?" And then, his frustration rising to the surface, translated his own message immediately into French: "Où est la masse de manoeuvre?"

Reynaud responded only, "Aucune!" ["None!"]

There was nothing and no one to stand between Hitler's forces and the French capital.

On June 3, planes with black swastikas flew over Paris, dropping bombs and laying waste to buildings, roads, and bridges. Rejewski, Zygalski, and Różycki watched in horror as their home was destroyed around them for the second time in less than a year.

Parisian streets were clogged with people fleeing the city. Cars were gridlocked, and people tried evacuating on foot, pushing what they could load into handcarts. The few trains that came through were mobbed with people who had slept at the stations, desperate for something to come along to take them away. Refugees from the north of France began flooding into Paris, adding to the crowds and chaos.

Rejewski, Zygalski, Różycki, Ciężki, Langer, and Palluth wouldn't get any help. The entire

French refugees fleeing the German invasion.
[Bundesarchiv, Bild 146–1971–083–01 / Tritschler / CC-BY-SA 3.0]

French government was evacuating, and there wasn't anything but a directive to leave.

"Everything was falling apart," Paul Paillole, the head of the Deuxième Bureau, remembered. "Nothing was planned. There was no order—it was every man for himself."

With no other instructions, Bertrand acted. At a depot, he commandeered—that is, he stole—a bus and a five-ton truck. Returning once again to PC Bruno, he loaded more than one hundred remaining French, Polish, and Spanish cryptographers, equipment, and files into these two vehicles. They blew up the radio monitoring stations.

"It is a miracle," he said. "I have been able to save my whole world—my archives and my Enigma."

On June 10, at 1:40 A.M., with Rejewski, Zygalski, Różycki, Ciężki, Langer, and Palluth among the passengers, the two vehicles headed south.

Incredibly, Bertrand and the codebreakers actually managed to set up their machines and decrypt messages as they traveled. At the town of La Ferté-Saint-Aubin, the decrypts told them of the heavy bombing in Paris and the Nazi celebrations of triumph. They worked for three days and packed up and traveled again—farther south.

In Bon-Encontre, in southern France, Bertrand contacted officials of the French general staff. He learned that Reynaud had resigned, and the new prime minister had signed an armistice with Hitler. The fighting was over, yet the terror had just begun.

Bertrand had no stomach for cooperation. The Nazi demand that all radio intelligence be turned over to them was ludicrous! He would never, *never* betray the codebreakers who looked to him to lead.

They had to get out of the country.

German soldiers in Paris.
[Bundesarchiv, Bild 101I-126–0350–26A / Fremke, Heinz / CC-BY-SA 3.0]

Hours later, Bertrand had a plan in action. North Africa was the closest, safest escape. At 3:25 P.M. on June 24, three planes landed in Oran, Algeria, carrying fifteen Poles and seven Spaniards.

PC Bruno was over, but French intelligence in exile was just getting started.

French prisoners of war march alongside German guards.
[Bundesarchiv, Bild 121–0404 / CC-BY-SA 3.0]

THIRTY-TWO

REFUSAL TO EXIT

June 1940—France

LEMOINE WAS A wanted man.

The Nazis were hunting him—they realized he had given them bad information when he was interrogated years before.

As the German Luftwaffe laid waste to Paris in Operation Paula, Paul Paillole rushed to Lemoine's apartment. "Suitcases cluttered the living room," he remembered. "A mass of papers were burning in the fireplace."

When Paillole told him to run, there was no argument from Lemoine. He knew he had to leave. Destroying evidence was the only reason he hadn't left sooner. He would go to Bordeaux and wait to be contacted at the national defense ministry.

Two weeks later, Henri Navarre, the same agent who had spoken with Hans-Thilo Schmidt in Switzerland, found Lemoine waiting in Bordeaux as promised.

"You must leave France," Navarre warned, echoing Paillole. "The enemy is looking for you. You're too vulnerable."

Navarre passed on mission orders for both Lemoine and his wife. They were to go to the French port of Saint-Jean-de-Luz and board a waiting British warship.

At 10 P.M., they came to the pier, now packed with people. Refugees from all walks of life, some with a ticket, but many, many more without, crowded the boat, desperate for passage to England and out of what was rapidly becoming Nazi-occupied land.

"When it was our turn [to board]," Lemoine recounted, "we were directed to a location on the bridge in the middle of a crowd. I asked an officer if we could find somewhere that was a bit more sheltered—for my wife."

The British officer swore at him, insulting the French and raging against the crowd.

It was too much for the harried Lemoine, used to being in control and living a life of ease.

"My blood was boiling," Lemoine remembered. "I told him in English that we would rather die in France than live and be insulted in England."

Lemoine and his wife got off the boat.

"It was nearly midnight," Lemoine remembered. "We left . . . and spent the night in the car. For the entire day of the 22nd [the next day] I sought in vain a way for us to board a French boat headed to Morocco."

But Navarre's offer had been a miracle that not even Lemoine could repeat. There were no spaces available. None to Morocco, no more to England. Everyone wanted out of France.

Lemoine and his wife turned around and headed back to Navarre and Paillole, who was masterminding the Deuxième Bureau's organization in exile.

It was another full day until Lemoine and his wife reached Paillole, and another night before the exhausted man could speak.

But after a night's rest, Lemoine, politely and gently this

time—unlike his response to the British naval officer—also refused Paillole's offer of shelter in Bordeaux.

Why, when everyone else seemed to be searching for a way out of France, had Lemoine become intent on staying?

"I have money and friends in Saint-Raphael," Lemoine explained.

But that was not the whole truth.

Paillole found the real answer as Lemoine reached into his bag to retrieve a folder. He looked down and, to his utter astonishment, saw in Lemoine's luggage "confidential documents, codes of various nationalities, unsigned passports of Dutch, Swedish, Danish nationalities, blank ID cards, stamps of all kinds . . . a trove of counterfeiting paraphernalia!"

There had always been "a certain amount of liberty regarding the source of his financial affairs," one agent at the Deuxième Bureau wrote, and now here was proof. Lemoine was profiting from the black market trade of counterfeit documents and information. He didn't want Paillole's "official" help and refuge; he wanted freedom and independence from the law—any law—to work as he always had: for his own gain.

Cheating at cards, turning assets to work for France, or selling secrets from spying—it was all the same to Lemoine, just different means of getting rich through deception.

There had been no news or contact from Asché.

EUROPE
1942

Bletchley
Park

London

UK

Paris

OCCUPIED FRANCE

UNOCCUPIED
(VICHY)
FRANCE

PORTUGAL

SPAIN

Poznaú

NAZI
GERMANY

Berlin

ITALY

Warsaw

ROMANIA

CONFIDENTIAL

PART 3

Sending Enigma messages

Winston Churchill

Women working at Bletchley Park

Wilhelm Canaris

THIRTY-THREE

YET ANOTHER HOME

June 16, 1940—Berlin, Germany

ADMIRAL WILHELM CANARIS, the head of the Abwehr (the German military intelligence agency), had been summoned to the Reich Chancellery, the seat of the German government. He waited in silence until Hermann Göring, one of Hitler's top cabinet members, came and gestured, without a word, calling Canaris in.

Hitler was standing. He made no welcome or overture but only thrust several papers at Canaris.

"There is a traitor in the bureau. We must discover the culprit fast—I intend for him to be punished regardless of his seniority," Hitler said. "Admiral, you will send me an account of your findings."

That was it. The meeting was over.

Silently, Göring escorted Canaris back to the waiting room. In a whisper, Göring explained, "It is clear there is a traitor, very well positioned, who has informed the diplomats of our offensive plans and the date of the attack in the West."

Göring gripped Canaris's shoulder. They knew there had been another leak earlier, as well. "The Führer, he too has not forgotten. Like me, he wonders if this is the same character that is running rampant among us."

Shaken and aghast, Canaris left. Back at his office, he looked through the papers. Secrets from planned attacks and entire conversations indicating time and place of invasions were littered across the pages.

The traitor's identity was in there somewhere, and Canaris was determined to find him out.

Fall 1940—France

The armistice had surrendered the entire nation of France to Germany, yet the Nazis only occupied the northern half of the country.

From a resort town named Vichy, a nominal French government that was actually under Nazi command led the French people. The Deuxième Bureau had ceased to exist, replaced by the Bureau des Menées Antinationales [Bureau of Anti-National Activities] under General Maxime Weygand.

Yet though the Nazis had won an armistice, the war for France was far from over.

In London, on June 18, 1940, former French brigadier general Charles de Gaulle spoke on BBC radio and called for resistance:

> *Honor, common sense, and the interests of the country require that all free Frenchmen, wherever they be, should continue the fight as best they may. . . .*
>
> *I call upon all Frenchmen who want to remain free to listen to my voice and follow me.*
>
> *Long live free France in honor and independence!*

General Weygand heard, and he was ready to answer.

Officially, Weygand worked for the new Vichy government.

Unofficially, Weygand put his resources and connections to work against the Nazis.

He summoned Paul Paillole and Bertrand. They had work to do.

What did Paillole know about farming? Nothing. Yet by the fall of 1940, he was leading the Travaux Ruraux [Rural Works].

It was a cover name. Travaux Ruraux became the Deuxième Bureau of the underground, free France, secretly collecting intelligence on the Nazis and their allies.

Less than two months after he had sent them to North Africa, Bertrand, under Paillole's direction, brought the codebreakers back.

Marian Rejewski became Pierre Ranaud, a high school teacher from Nantes. Henryk Zygalski became René Sergent. Jerzy Różycki was remolded into Julien Rouget. Along with thirteen other Polish men (including Langer, Ciężki, and Palluth), seven Spanish codebreakers, and seven French staff, they were given new, fake backgrounds as businessmen, clerks, and craftsmen.

It was incredibly risky, and over in England, Denniston was furious that Bertrand did not immediately send the men to Bletchley Park, where they would be, relatively, safer. But Bertrand would not give up his prized team.

For the Polish codebreakers, work went on at a feverish pace throughout the winter and into the spring and summer of 1941. There was always more to understand, more to translate and decipher. Bertrand kept a close eye on them and reported often to Paillole.

For his part, Paillole had bigger worries on his hands. Lemoine had never left France.

THIRTY-FOUR

U-BOAT PERIL

Winter 1941—England

NOW THAT HE had Paris, Hitler did not stop; he ordered the Nazis to attack. In the south, battles raged in Greece, Libya, and Egypt. In the east, more than half a million German soldiers were amassing on the Romanian-Soviet border to occupy the Balkans before beginning Operation Barbarossa, the invasion of the USSR. But in the west, where ocean replaced roads and mountains, it was Dönitz's battle that raged.

Dönitz had said he needed three hundred U-boats to make England surrender. In the winter of 1941, he had sixty-five. Of those, fewer than twenty U-boats were patrolling the ocean at any one time.

It didn't seem like much, only a few handfuls, really. Yet, even with these paltry few submarines, England felt the threat.

"With everybody killing and fighting each other, and sinking each others' ships, and crops not getting planted, and labor shortage everywhere due to men being soldiers instead of growing food—how soon will there be famine over the world?" wrote Nella Last, a British housewife, in her journal.

Rationing had seen that everyone could find calories, even if "cheese, eggs, onions, oranges, luxury fruits and vegetables are practically unobtainable," wrote journalist Maggie Joy Blunt. But the war was far from over, and they already faced shortages. It wasn't hard to read what was coming: if the fighting lasted much longer, England could starve.

At the stores and markets, "grim-faced women queue and push—and hurry off to another queue when served," wrote Last. What had once been taken for granted was now prized and treasured.

And that was the result of Dönitz working with less than a third of the U-boat fleet he was aiming to build.

So much of what Britain needed came from somewhere else. The island nation was dependent on imported food.

"The only thing that ever really frightened me during the war was the U-boat peril," wrote Prime Minister Winston Churchill.

If only twenty U-boats could cause this much damage, what would happen when Dönitz got his hands on more?

At Bletchley Park, more spider bombes arrived as fast as the factory in Letchworth could produce them. Hut 11, hastily built over the winter, housed six bombes by March.

The codebreakers in Hut 6 who worked on the German army/air force net had enough cribs to keep the bombes busy. Day and night, they ran, spitting out settings and allowing the codebreakers to read messages.

But in Hut 8, the German naval Enigma didn't have a single offering for the machine.

They hadn't broken any new settings since November.

THIRTY-FIVE

SOMALI

*March 4, 1941—Norwegian archipelago of the Lofoten Islands,
north of the Arctic Circle*

BLUE-EYED, THIRTY-YEAR-OLD BRITISH lieutenant Marshall
George Clitheroe Warmington, signals officer on board the destroyer
HMS *Somali*, watched as the Norwegian island of Skrova slid into
view. It had been a cloudy night with snow obscuring the stars, but
by the early morning hours, the sea had calmed and the wind was
down to a light breeze in the freezing air.

The *Somali* was hunting. The ship and four other destroyers were
escorting two troop carrier ships, all bent on wreaking havoc on
the Nazi occupation of Norway: they planned to destroy fish factories (and the precious vitamins a fish-based diet contained), capture
Norwegian collaborators with the Nazis, and provide an escape for
any locals who wished to fight in the larger war.

Skrova, rising barely 921 feet above the sea and only a mile long,
wasn't important enough to warrant a stop. All the British ships had
to do was pass by undetected.

They almost made it.

The little bump of an island had already risen and was falling away from the *Somali*'s view when harbor lights snapped
off, plunging the surrounding land and water into darkness. The

Germans occupying the island had realized their enemy was close.

The *Somali* picked up speed and rushed to escort the troop carriers to their points of attack, only a handful of miles away.

Then, turning back to keep patrol, the *Somali* passed Skrova once again.

The Somali.
[Wikimedia Commons]

The island had fallen behind the British ship when a tiny trawler-turned-patrol-boat—armed only with a small gun at the bow (in front) and a heavy machine gun aft (in back)—shot out of its harbor. Though she was small, she was coming to do her duty.

At two miles apart, *Somali* fired. The shots whizzed high, serving as a warning only and doing no damage.

Then, with "all the guts in the world," Warmington remembered, little *Krebs* actually fired back!

The closest any of her shots came to doing damage was a hole in one of the British warship's flags. But it was enough to enrage the *Somali*'s commander. His next rounds did not miss.

The first shot detonated an ammunition pile. The second shot exploded in the wheelhouse. The third shot demolished the boiler room.

The *Krebs* was finished. She slowly spun in circles in the water as smoke billowed out from the boat. Survivors jumped overboard and began fighting for their lives in the freezing sea.

On board the *Somali*, the second in command, Lieutenant Henry A. Stuart-Menteth, had already seen action and been wounded in the war. In 1940, he had been pulled unconscious from the water and brought to a German hospital. They had saved his life (and then left him behind when they fled from attacking British troops). Now he watched as the enemy struggled in the waters below his own ship.

"They hauled me out," he reminded himself, and he threw a net over the side of the destroyer and began pulling the German men up onto the *Somali*'s deck with his own hands.

For a while, it looked like the *Krebs* had been beached on one of the smaller islands. But when it started to drift again, still burning, into the open water, Warmington noticed a white flag, a symbol of surrender, being waved desperately on its deck.

A few minutes later, guns cocked and ready, Warmington and his boarding party stepped onto the *Krebs*. The five men still alive offered no resistance.

The captain was dead; he was lying in the wheelhouse, killed by the *Somali*'s second shot. Warmington went into his cabin. Papers were strewn around the room. There was a gridded map, documents labeled SECRET, and a locked drawer.

"If it's locked," he said to himself, "there must be something there."

He pulled out his gun once again. Warmington had seen plenty of action movies, and he prepared to shoot the lock off the drawer. He looked away, pulled the trigger, and for a horrible moment panicked as the bullet ricocheted around the room; suddenly he was in danger of being killed by his own shot.

The bullet eventually stopped, and the trick worked. Warmington's instinctive reaction to the drawer had been correct. Pulling it open, he found a small wooden box. Inside, there were two discs with grooved edges and letters around the sides.

By this time, Warmington had already been on the *Krebs* for forty-five minutes, and the *Somali* began signaling him to come back. Quickly, he shoved the discs, along with all the papers he could find, into bags.

Mere days after that, the discs and the documents were handed over at Bletchley Park. It would turn out to be invaluable information. But there were other puzzle pieces yet to be found before the codebreakers could see the whole picture.

THIRTY-SIX

WEATHER SHIPS

Spring 1941—Bletchley Park, England

HARRY HINSLEY NO longer turned a hand-crank phone for a chance to speak with someone at the Admiralty. By the spring of 1941, naval officers at the Admiralty were calling *him*. Sporting the most fashionable haircuts done in swanky West End boroughs of London, sauntering the city in bespoke Burberry suits on his way to meetings chaired by Churchill himself, Hinsley had come a long way from the disheveled college student spending the summer with his German girlfriend on a strict budget.

Traffic analysis, Hinsley's insight that there was usable information surrounding the undecipherable Enigma messages, was now an established source of intelligence. And he was about to have another thought that would change the course of the war.

Hinsley was at his desk, shuffling through piles of papers when an errant "passing thought" occurred to him like lightning: German weather reports were enciphered with a naval Enigma machine.

These weather reports were transmitted regularly by weather ships that traveled well-known routes on deployments that lasted as much as two months. The weather ships must each carry at least one month's worth—and maybe even two months' worth!—of codebooks. And best of all, they were very lightly armed.

"Good God, this must be right!" he thought after a "mad moment" processing his idea.

His contacts at the Admiralty's Operational Intelligence Center agreed.

May 7, 1941—northern Atlantic Ocean, halfway between Iceland and Norway

The afternoon of Wednesday, May 7, 1941, was only slightly above freezing. Barely two months had passed since the destroyer *Somali* had fought in the Lofoten archipelago. Now, with a light breeze sending gentle ripples over the calm waters, the *Somali* headed north once more, hunting once again.

The *Somali* and three other destroyers were set ten miles apart to comb the area for weather ships. Visibility was only seven or eight miles, making it harder to spot a ship. But, then again, the poor visibility was good cover for the Royal Navy vessels as well.

Just after 5 P.M., Lieutenant Warmington saw smoke over the water.

Rattlers, "a series of short noises like a big alarm clock," one sailor remembered, called everyone to their battle stations. The *Somali* put on speed and raced toward the little ship rising out of the horizon.

When they were three miles apart, the *Somali* and one other destroyer that had joined the chase opened fire. The small weather ship did not even attempt a defense.

Warmington readied the boarding party as his ship approached the small German one. They jumped from the destroyer down onto the deck of the weather ship. The only gunfire was when one British sailor accidentally shot himself in the foot. Most of the German sailors had already abandoned ship, fleeing in lifeboats as the *Somali* had approached and sent towers of water caving over her decks.

Warmington turned over a few pieces of paper, shuffling through the debris that was left behind, but there was nothing worth taking in the radio room.

The codebooks were gone.

In the moments before they were boarded, the weather ship's crew had crammed the current keys and their entire Enigma machine into a canvas bag created for just one purpose: to sink materials quickly and absolutely.

The Germans had learned their lesson after *Schiff 26/Polares*, when secrets had been given up simply because their duffel bag had floated and Gunner Foord had jumped into the water to seize it. Now a lead bottom, sewn directly into the bag, ensured that it would sink and the water-soluble ink would be rendered unreadable.

Luckily, as Warmington prowled around the communications office, another officer was climbing on board. Captain Jasper Haines wore civilian clothes, but he was a highly trained officer with a specialty in information recovery, sent specifically to the weather ship ambush in order to gather Enigma codebooks. He knew exactly what to look for and where he would likely find it. As Warmington dug through scraps of paper in the radio room, Haines dashed past him. Mere moments later, he returned to Warmington, triumphant.

The crew of the weather ship had disposed of the current Enigma keys, but they hadn't had time or hadn't thought to get rid of the keys for other codes they carried. These codes, though not at first glance related to Enigma, would prove to be an important part of the codebreakers' puzzle.

Meanwhile, sailors on the *Somali* were rescuing German sailors, pulling them out of the water and sending ladders down to life-boats.

"What's the name of the ship?" the captain of the *Somali* shouted out, not even knowing who he had ambushed.

"Wie heist deine Schiff?" translated the *Somali's* physician and surgeon.

"*München*," the sailors replied.

An hour and a half after the *Somali* first sighted the *München*, the British destroyer turned back toward British port, escorting her prize.

As she headed home, the Admiralty instructed the *Somali* to broadcast a message. They knew the Germans would undoubtedly listen in, which was exactly what the Admiralty wanted them to do. Because the *Somali* was going to lie:

"One of our patrols operating in northern waters encountered the *München*, a German armed trawler. Fire was opened, and the crew of the *München* then abandoned and scuttled their ship. They were subsequently rescued and made prisoner."

It was a fake message, sent only to mislead the Nazis.

The truth was that the *München* had never been scuttled. She had been boarded, raided, and her crew captured and isolated in order to prevent the truth from reaching German ears. But, if the Nazis found out that a weather ship was in British hands, they could realize that their Enigma cipher was in jeopardy and then they might change the whole system. The codebreakers needed the Germans to believe that they had not found any new information. The weather ship was worthless unless the Nazis believed that the *München* and its secrets had been destroyed, unless the Nazis believed the lie.

May 9, 1941—northern Atlantic Ocean, near Iceland

The *Somali* had been on a hunt for Enigma intelligence; Captain Jasper Haines had known exactly what to search for. But most of the time, it was luck, quick thinking, and a thorough pillaging of a U-boat that brought back what was so desperately needed.

Such was the case when *U-110* was forced to surrender after attacking the Allied 3rd Escort Group near Iceland. Commanding officer Joe Baker-Cresswell of HMS *Bulldog* and his men had never trained or drilled on operations to seize a U-boat, but that was not going to stand in their way.

"Organize a boarding party instantly," he commanded. "The sublieutenant will be in charge."

Down the length of the ship, shouts summoned the sublieutenant, David E. Balme, to the bridge: "Hey, you sub! Away you go!"

"Your job," the captain told Balme when he arrived, "is to secure all important papers, ciphers, charts—anything that you can find."

Balme was barely twenty years old. He had "a mischievous look and a twinkle in his eye, [and] was once characterized as a type who made girls happy when he came ashore," wrote one historian. But none of that would help him face the deep unknown of a German U-boat.

Balme gathered eight men and a few guns, grenades, and gas masks from the *Bulldog*, and then took a twenty-seven-foot, five-oared whaler across the water.

He had never climbed down a conning tower ladder before. It was almost suicidal, he thought, for someone inexperienced to do it while holding a gun. So he holstered his revolver and prepared to face the unknown without any ready defense.

Was the boat booby-trapped? Were the Germans biding their

time, ready to ambush the first man down? There was no way to tell if anyone was waiting for him below. Was a vent open with seawater pouring in, about to plunge the U-boat beneath the waves?

Balme climbed down alone.

Inside, all the lights were on. No Germans appeared. No shots rang out, and no rush of water filled his ears. The German sailors had left in a hurry, without any strategy. A plate of shrimp still lay out in the radio room. Balme called the rest of his men down into the U-boat.

The British sailors formed a human chain, passing up every note, book, log, and chart they could find. In the radio room, they noted the settings of the transmitters and receivers. They recognized a typewriter-looking-thing as a cipher device, though they did not know it was an Enigma machine. And that, too, they unscrewed from the table and passed up.

HMS U-110 *and* Bulldog.
[Wikimedia Commons]

When the *Bulldog* had finished rescuing German sailors out of the water, and Balme had finished gathering information and equipment inside, Baker-Cresswell began towing *U-110* back to the British naval harbor at Scapa Flow. But the U-boat was leaking, and she sank rapidly the morning after the attack.

Crushed, Baker-Cresswell consoled himself: "At least I've got the cipher."

He had gotten more than he realized. In Scapa Flow, two men with a single briefcase between them boarded the *Bulldog*. They were stunned, ecstatic when they saw the documents that Balme had salvaged.

"I never thought we'd get any of this!" one exclaimed.

The two men photographed every page of the documents. That way, even if there was an air raid that destroyed the originals or if the plane that would carry the men and the documents back to Bletchley Park crashed on the way, there would be multiple records.

Balme and the *Bulldog* had found codebreaking gold.

As they left the *Bulldog*, one of the intelligence officers, Lieutenant Allon Bacon, sought out Baker-Cresswell.

"Never mind about losing the *U-110*," he consoled the commander. "From our point of view, it was a good thing, as we can now keep all this quiet. For God's sake never breathe a word about this to anyone."

June 28, 1941—northern Atlantic Ocean, northeast of Iceland

The German weather ship *Lauenburg* had run, but she hadn't fought. When the British ship *Tartar* closed in and fired warning shots, all but two of the *Lauenburg*'s crew piled into lifeboats and simply rowed as far away as they could go.

By the time Lieutenant T. Hugh P. Wilson arrived from the *Tartar* with his boarding party, the last two Germans on board the *Lauenburg* had ensured that the Enigma machine was gone, and the furnace was hot from papers and charts.

But the two German crewmen who had stayed behind on the

weather ship hadn't had time to get rid of it all. The floor was strewn with abandoned notes and scribbles on pieces of paper.

"For God's sake, man, look at all this material," cried Lieutenant Bacon, who had attended the raid as intelligence officer. "Pack it up!"

"What?" replied Wilson, pointing to the scraps on the floor and desk. "All this rubbish?"

Yes, Bacon wanted it all.

By the time they were done, he had thirteen mail sacks of documents, all headed to Bletchley Park.

THIRTY-SEVEN

TIDES TURN

July 1, 1941—Bletchley Park, England

"HERE IT IS," said intelligence officer Lieutenant Allon Bacon, rather unceremoniously for the occasion.

He dumped his canvas bag onto the table in front of the codebreakers, the contents spilling out like pieces to a giant jigsaw puzzle. The codebreakers took a look at the papers, and not five minutes later, every single one had rushed back to Hut 8.

Enigma was about to fall.

That afternoon, the codebreakers read German naval Enigma messages for the first time in nine months. By the next day, they were reading messages within three hours of their arrival at Bletchley Park.

Information from *Krebs*, seized due to the quick thinking of Lieutenant Warmington, allowed the codebreakers to reconstruct the bigram tables. The weather ship *München*, as Hinsley had hoped, provided all the naval Enigma settings for the entire month of June. From the *Lauenburg*, they not only discovered all of the settings for July, but they also found out that new bigram tables were being used across the fleet. Luckily, the *Lauenburg* gave them those tables, too.

Every bit they read helped them understand the Enigma system better, and they began to discover patterns and routines to messages. When their current set of cribs ran out, these insights would enable the codebreakers to keep working.

The codebreakers learned other procedures, too.

Within the naval Enigma net, the most sensitive, classified information was sent using a special procedure called Offizier messages: for officers' eyes only. The Bletchley Park cryptographers had not even understood the process of *how* these messages were encrypted, much less developed the tools to break the cipher.

Until the capture of *U-110* provided the manual that explained it all.

The codebreakers in Hut 8 broke their first Offizier messages not long after Bacon delivered the documents.

The bombes ran day and night, alternating between Hut 6 and Hut 8 intelligence, spitting out keys for the German army/air force or naval nets, whichever had the greatest need. On land, in the air, or on the sea—Britain now had information for every front. The only question that remained was how long it would last.

Summer 1941—Berlin, Germany

"It seems that the British ships are getting around the locations picked out for attacks," wrote Dönitz in his war diary. "This leads one to suspect that our ambush points are known to the enemy."

Not only were the British ships evading the U-boat attacks, thanks to the codebreakers, but intelligence from Enigma messages was helping them take down German ships as well.

That summer, the Royal Navy captured *U-570* and the German supply ship *Gedania*. Later, *U-68* and *U-111* narrowly escaped

British capture, but only after an ambush where British destroyers sank the Dutch ship the Germans were escorting. In the month of June alone, Enigma intelligence was responsible for six of the eight German ships taken down by the British navy.

Back in Berlin, Dönitz's doubts continued to mount. After every capture and near miss, he asked whether Enigma was secure. He wrote in his war diary that the capture of *U-570* especially was a "depressing event."

Each time Dönitz asked, Vice Admiral Erhard Maertens, the head of the German navy's communication service, replied that Enigma was safe.

After *U-570*, Maertens wrote to Dönitz that "everything suggests that the crew had the chance to destroy at least one of the secret cipher documents. [And if this is true] it would be impossible for the enemy to read our messages."

Later, Maertens wrote bluntly, "Our cipher does not appear to have been broken."

Dönitz let his doubts rest. He didn't alter the "unbreakable" German code.

THIRTY-EIGHT

INTERLUDE

Fall 1941—Bletchley Park, England

FOR A WHILE, life at Bletchley Park went on at a regular, routine pace.

The sheer volume of work was staggering. Everywhere, Bletchley Park was increasing its personnel. Women were recruited for the big room clerical work and to run the cipher machines. New code-breakers were hired, too, to work on and improve the tools that Turing, Clarke, Welchman, Hinsley, and others had developed.

Wrens attending bombes at Eastcote outstation.
[Bletchley Park]

As more bombes were produced, GC&CS began installing them in outposts across the country. Bletchley Park itself didn't have room for all these machines, and it was far safer to spread out the bombes. If Bletchley Park was ever destroyed in an air raid, there would still be bombes at other sites to continue the work.

The codebreakers stayed at Bletchley Park and formed the cribs and bombe menus. Wrens—members of the Women's Royal Naval Service—physically operated and maintained the machines.

At first, "it was doubted if the girls could do the work," one senior man remembered.

They could. And they did.

By the end of the war, more than two hundred bombes were up and running, cared for by 1,676 Wrens. The Wrens were up to the task, but it was grueling, exhausting, and arduous labor to physically decrypt Enigma.

"The back of the machine defies description," remembered one Wren. "A mass of dangling plugs ... and a multitude of wires, every one of which had to be meticulously adjusted with tweezers to make sure the electrical circuits did not short."

"You had to be accurate as a bombe operator," another Wren recalled. "You didn't have to be a crossword puzzler or a Greek scholar, but you did have to be incredibly accurate. . . . Anything you did wrong caused a short circuit."

And yet they did it, day after day, night after night. Standing, moving wires in adjustments of mere millimeters for eight hours straight.

*Miles of wires along the back of the bombes
required meticulous attention and care by the Wrens.*
[Richard Gillin via Flickr]

When they did get sick—they called it "the burnout"—they wouldn't let on what was wrong.

A letter from one doctor treating a Wren implored her boss to help find out the cause of her malaise. The girl "will not divulge the smallest detail of what she does [for work], even though it is against her own interests," the doctor wrote.

Her GC&CS supervisor wrote back, "There is nothing peculiar in her silence. That is perfectly correct in her behavior—in fact it is highly commendable."

If a Wren became sick, she rested as best she could. Then she went back to work. No less than the codebreakers themselves, the war depended on them.

The army of codebreakers was increasing its numbers, too.

Secrecy, an absolute rule, meant that as few people should be involved with Enigma as possible. Yet the volume of work meant that many more people were needed.

Already, the original codebreakers had become legends, and their groundbreaking work was part myth, part miracle.

One new codebreaker, Irving John Good, started his time at Bletchley Park by poring over a manual explaining Enigma. Besides being rather hastily and poorly written, it only detailed the current methods of breaking the code; there was nothing about the history of cracking Enigma or means of discovery.

"How on earth did we get the wiring of the rotors?" Good asked Turing and Clarke, who were working together close by where he was reading.

Turing's reply was brief and not entirely helpful: "Perhaps the Poles."

"Perhaps a pinch?" Good asked.

"Something like that," Turing replied, turning back to his work with Clarke.

Clearly, that was the end of the conversation.

Bletchley Park needed more help; they needed more people. But there were limits to what any one person needed to know.

THIRTY-NINE

CHURCHILL

Fall 1941—Bletchley Park, England

ENIGMA INTELLIGENCE ARRIVED daily for Prime Minister Winston Churchill. He had great respect for information obtained through codebreaking; during WWI, Churchill had helped form Room 40, the precursor to GC&CS. Now, in the throes of WWII, he kept the key to the beige box containing his Enigma briefs on his personal keyring.

In the fall of 1941, Churchill decided it was time to pay the codebreakers a visit. He arrived at Bletchley Park for a tour on September 6.

Gordon Welchman, in Hut 6, had been told to prepare a ten-minute speech for the prime minister. But when the day arrived, Churchill was running late.

"Five minutes, Welchman," Commander Edward Travis, a military officer who helped oversee Enigma decryption, whispered loudly as he led Churchill's tour into the hut.

"I would like to make three points," Welchman began, rushing rather more than he had planned. Even still, he only made it through two ideas before Travis interrupted.

"That's enough, Welchman," Travis said as he began ushering the tour on.

Churchill, undeterred, loved hearing from the codebreakers and was enjoying himself. "I think there was a third point, Welchman," he urged, giving the codebreaker a wink.

Travis waited; Welchman finished his speech.

"Sir, I would like to present John Herivel, who was responsible for breaking the [army/air force] German Enigma last year."

Herivel, whose tip did in fact lead to some of the first breaks in Enigma, was taken entirely by surprise. "On hearing my name spoken by Welchman in this totally unexpected manner, I turned automatically to the right to find myself gazing straight into the eyes of the Prime Minister!"

When Welchman had finished, Churchill's tour moved on. At the end of the day, he made a short speech to the entire staff of Bletchley Park.

"He stood rather uneasily for a moment—for it was a miserable dark day with a cold wind," Herivel remembered.

"You all look very innocent—one would not think you knew anything secret," Churchill joked. But with admiration and gratitude, he lauded the whole park as "the geese that lay the golden eggs—and never cackle."

The codes they broke and the intelligence they gathered would mean nothing if the secret got out.

Secrecy meant keeping the staff at Bletchley Park to a very minimum. Yet what Bletchley Park really needed was more codebreakers.

At the beginning of the war, Welchman and others had simply recruited their friends and the people their friends recommended. Without much trouble, they hired the best minds they could find. But by 1941, that was over.

Just as the bombes and other tools became capable of actually breaking Enigma's ciphers, the manpower to drive the work dried up. Other efforts—like research into nuclear energy and radio and radar technology—needed geniuses, too. "Men of the professor type" were rationed like any other limited, necessary item during the war.

Thankfully Churchill's visit made the four "wicked uncles" of Bletchley Park—Welchman, Turing, Alexander, and Milner-Barry—bold. One month later, they wrote to Churchill directly.

SECRET AND CONFIDENTIAL

Prime Minster only Hut 6 and Hut 8

(Bletchley Park)

21st October 1941

Dear Prime Minister,

Some weeks ago you paid us the honor of a visit, and we believe that you regard our work as important. . . . We think, however, that you ought to know that this work is being held up, and in some cases not being done at all, principally because we cannot get sufficient staff to deal with it.

. . . The effect of this is that the finding of the naval keys is being delayed at least twelve hours every day.

. . . We have written this letter entirely on our own initiative. . . . We have felt that we should be failing in our duty if we did not draw your attention to the facts and to the effects which they are having and must continue to have on our work, unless immediate action is taken.

We are, Sir, Your obedient servants,

A. M. Turing

W. G. Welchman

C. H. O'D. Alexander

P. S. Milner-Barry

Churchill read the letter on October 22. Immediately, he issued one of his most famous Action This Day memos:

Make sure they have all they want on extreme priority and report to me that this has been done.

Churchill's "Action This Day" memo answering the request of the Bletchley Park codebreakers.
[The National Archives]

His injunction came just in time. No one was prepared for what was coming next.

FORTY

SHARK IN THE WATER

Winter 1942—Bletchley Park, England

"ON FEBRUARY 1, 1942, the blow fell," wrote Hugh Alexander.

It was a brilliant design: where the naval Enigma machine had once held three rotors, in the same space, it now fit four.

The old three-rotor setup had 17,576 possible combinations of different letters. The four-rotor machine had 456,976.

At Bletchley Park, the only good thing they could say about the change was that it applied to U-boats alone. All German surface ships, and U-boats when they were in coastal waters, still used the three-rotor Enigma.

But out in the ocean, prowling on the hunt as a wolfpack, the U-boats used all four rotors. The codebreakers named the new net Shark, quite possibly because they knew the four-rotor setup would lead to bloodshed in the water.

There had been some hints—barely— in the months leading up to the change.

A four-rotor Enigma.
[LukaszKatlewa via Wikimedia Commons]

A few decoded Enigma messages implied the possibility of a fourth rotor. A few German operators had gotten sloppy.

In December 1941, the codebreakers had found a message that just wouldn't translate. They had found the keys, and the bombes had broken the rest of the messages for that day, but no matter what they did to this particular message, the letters had remained meaningless.

That is, it was meaningless until they read the message that followed: "E bar 551 [the previous message] deciphers with setting B."

Something was different about the Enigma that had sent the unreadable message. "Setting B"—whatever that was—was new.

Using information in the message known as E bar 551 and other intercepts, the codebreakers could—and did—solve for the wiring inside the new rotor.

But it wasn't enough.

It was *possible* to break Shark messages; they could make the bombes work for the four-rotor setup. The problem was time.

"An average Shark job would have taken 50 to 100 times as long as an average Air or Army job so that it would have been a moot point whether it would have been worthwhile even if possible," Alexander wrote.

There simply weren't enough bombes in existence to break both Shark and the German army/air force nets. Not only that, but Bletchley Park still had to contend with the non-U-boat naval traffic. This net, now named Dolphin, still needed to be broken and read daily.

One lucky break for the codebreakers came on March 14. On that day, an identical message was transmitted through both the Shark and Dolphin nets.

Dönitz had been promoted to admiral.

He sent out the announcement to the entire navy, using the exact same message on all nets. His pride made him overlook the cardinal rule of codebreaking: never repeat something that you want kept secret.

Yet even with this perfect crib, it took an obscene amount of time to decipher the Shark settings. Six bombes worked nonstop for seventeen days just to find the answers.

Harry Hinsley later remembered, "the basic problem was that Dönitz was not promoted every day and that alternative god-sends were few and far between."

The codebreakers would never be handed another crib like that again, and the bombes could not keep up. Bletchley Park was effectively blind, and all the U-boat traffic in the Atlantic went dark once again.

PART 4

Jadwiga and Antoni Palluth

Monument to Jerzy Różycki

Turing's math notes on theory of Enigma

HMS Petard

Relevant parts of alphabets

1	2	3	4	5	6	7	8	9
AU	AR	RV	ND	AR	GL	KX NY UB	LH	AH

10	11	12	13	14	15	16	17	18
RV	GT	LP	NE	LU	CK RN OU			

19	20	21	22	23	24	25	26
DC FR ND	RL	BL	AV	VT	QL		

Fig 65. Illustrating the kind of position at which the Spider will stop. Here the input letter may be supposed to be E and the relay which closed R. The Stecker values of the letters, which are consequences of the hypothesis ER are written against the letters. There are contradictions such as Z/L, W/L:

FORTY-ONE

LOSSES AND LACONIA
Winter 1941 to summer 1942—United States

"**YESTERDAY, DECEMBER 7,** 1941—a date which will live in infamy—the United States of America was suddenly and deliberately attacked by naval and air forces of the Empire of Japan. . . ." President Franklin D. Roosevelt addressed the United States Congress just after noon on December 8.

The day before, at 7:55 A.M., 360 planes and 5 midget submarines had struck the American naval base at Pearl Harbor. Ninety minutes after it began, the Japanese attack was over, leaving more than two thousand Americans dead or dying.

Immediately after his speech, a joint session of the US Congress granted President Roosevelt's request to declare war on Japan. Germany, an ally of Japan, then declared war on the United States on December 11, 1941. Within weeks, there were German U-boats off the Atlantic coast of the US.

"Hit them like you're beating a drum. Attack on! Sink them! You mustn't come home empty-handed," one U-boat commander ordered his crew.

The United States was entirely unprepared to deal with the German naval forces. While the coast of Europe went silently dark every night, the eastern seaboard of the US remained lit, silhouetting the warships in its waters, giving the U-boats easy targets.

Dönitz was incredulous that an enemy could be so obvious:

The coast was not blacked-out, and the towns were a blaze of bright lights. . . . It did not take the U-boats long to work out a very effective routine. By day they lay on the bottom at depths of anything from 150 to 400 feet and a few miles from the shipping routes. At dusk they approached the coast submerged and when darkness fell [they then] surfaced in the middle of the stream of shipping to deliver their attacks.

When "the obvious defense measure" of darkening the US coast was first proposed, one American naval officer remembered that "squawks went up all the way from Atlantic City to southern Florida that 'the tourist season would be ruined.' . . . Ships were sunk and seamen drowned in order that the citizenry might enjoy business and pleasure as usual."

Eventually, the US navy set up an escort system with military ships protecting civilian cargo and passenger vessels, just as the British navy had done in the northern Atlantic and Mediterranean. As it became harder to attack Americans off the East Coast, the U-boats were recalled to Europe.

Even then, the decimation did not stop—it just moved.

In the second half of 1942, the Nazis sunk 2.6 million tons of Allied goods; only six hundred thousand tons had been sunk in the same time period the previous year while the codebreakers were reading the German naval Enigma. In the freezing waters of the

Atlantic Ocean, sailors died and went down with the food their families needed to survive, the coal to keep their children from freezing, the fuel to keep Allied planes in the air, and the ammunition to keep fighting.

At Bletchley Park, intercepts piled up, and there was no way of reading them. The information was *right there* on the desks in front of them, but once again the codebreakers could not get inside.

Back in the States, American intelligence was given the go-ahead for a project costing around two million dollars (about $40 million in 2022) to produce a bombe capable of breaking the Enigma cipher. They had decided to build their own, because the British certainly weren't sharing.

It was the same story GC&CS had told Bertrand and the Americans before: Enigma intelligence was too precious to spread around.

In one letter, Stewart Menzies, the head of British intelligence agency MI6, had written to Churchill, "I greatly doubt the enemy being for a moment deceived should there be any indiscretion in the USA. That this might occur cannot be ruled out as the Americans are not in any sense as security minded as one would wish . . ."

The American decision to commit such a sum of money to build a bombe of their own, however, convinced British intelligence to open the doors ever so slightly. Slowly, reluctantly, GC&CS admitted the Americans into the Enigma inner circle. Harry Hinsley flew to Washington, DC, to finalize an exchange of information, and Alan Turing went to Dayton, Ohio, to help the Americans design and build their bombes.

(Even then, though, hostilities between the two intelligence agencies were far from over. Hinsley negotiated an agreement for naval Enigma nets only. The British trusted the Americans even less with the air force/army net. It got so bad that, while in the States, Turing was actually locked out of his office until things could get resolved.)

Yet the teamwork between the two countries, when it did happen, couldn't solve everything. Even with Turing's help in Dayton, the fastest that the American bombes could possibly be manufactured and ready to work was February 1943. That was months away, leaving plenty of time for the destruction of Allied ships in the Atlantic.

Fall 1942—Germany

From the start, Dönitz had argued that he needed three hundred U-boats to deliver a "mortal blow" to Britain. Finally, in August 1942, he had them.

On September 17, he issued a directive, called the Laconia Order, effective immediately, to the entire U-boat fleet:

> *All attempts to rescue the crews of sunken ships will cease forthwith. . . . Such activities are a contradiction of the primary object of war, namely the destruction of enemy ships and their crews.*

The Nazi fleet was ready, and they would show no mercy.

FORTY-TWO

U-559 AND PETARD

October 30, 1942—Mediterranean Sea

BRITISH LIEUTENANT-COMMANDER Mark Thornton, a gruff man decorated for bravery in battle, demanded instantaneous obedience from his crew on HMS *Petard*. He tested them, too.

He ordered his men to keep a constant watch for submarines, whether they were on duty or not. If he happened upon anyone who was being inattentive, he pelted them with whatever was closest to him at the time—chalk, stones, or even teacups. At one point, he ordered his officers to jump into the sea and swim around the ship during a storm, just to prove their compliance to his demands. (Luckily, someone eventually managed to convince him they might all die before his orders were carried out.)

It fell to Thornton's second in command, First Lieutenant Tony Fasson, to soothe many wounded feelings and bruised egos after the commander's bullying.

Though Thornton and Fasson disagreed on how best to manage a ship, they were united on a different front: both were obsessed with capturing a U-boat and seizing its codebooks.

For months, they discussed, argued, and planned how best to get at the German codes. They had both been firsthand witnesses to the destruction in the Atlantic, and more than taking down a single U-boat, they wanted a part in decimating the entire fleet.

When the *Petard* spotted a U-boat on the afternoon of October 30, 1942, everyone knew the chase was on.

For ten hours, *U-559* ping-ponged between shallow water and the depths. The *Petard's* sonarman, Ken Lacroix, raked the U-boat with ASDIC, but churned-up debris choked the sonar's signals every time the U-boat dropped down to the seafloor.

The *Petard's* sailors needed a way to force *U-559* to stay closer to the surface. So, to make their depth charges more effective, to reach farther down to where the U-boat was hiding, the British sailors rammed soap into the depth-charge's regulator, fooling the weapon into detonating far deeper than designed.

The trick worked. Explosions wounded *U-559*, and the U-boat moved to shallower waters, where the ASDIC signal on the *Petard* became stronger.

As the night wore on, the Nazi U-boat crew became light-headed from carbon dioxide poisoning the air inside their vessel. Hissing pierced through the rumble of engines as their pressurized air escaped through cracks from the depth charges. Soon, water began leaking in, and the rear of the U-boat sank lower than the bow. Hans Heidtmann, commander of *U-559*, ordered men to the front of the boat in an attempt to level it out. But their efforts didn't amount to anything. *U-559* was sinking.

Using the only option left, Heidtmann ordered the water blown out of the diving tanks; lighter air immediately replaced the water, and the more-buoyant U-boat shot straight to the surface. The men abandoned ship.

On the *Petard*, it was Gordon Connell's job to lead the boarding party. From the bridge, Thornton shouted down that he should dive into the sea immediately and swim to the U-boat. Obediently, Connell began removing his clothes.

Fasson tapped his shoulder. "You're not going. You're married," he said, and he charged forward to the bow of the ship, stripping his clothes as he went.

As Fasson ran past the sonarman, he shouted, "Come on, Lacroix, it's your sub!"

Fasson and Lacroix, along with sailor Colin Grazier and fifteen-year-old canteen assistant Tommy Brown, who had lied about his age to join the navy, jumped naked from the deck of the *Petard* and swam a short distance to the ailing U-boat.

Fasson, then Grazier, then Lacroix, then Brown went down the conning tower ladder as Thornton yelled at them through the *Petard*'s loud-hailer to be sure to search the pockets of anyone they came across.

"The lights were out," remembered Brown. "The First Lieutenant had a torch [flashlight]. The water was not very high but rising gradually all the time. . . . First Lieutenant was down there with a machine-gun . . . which he was using to smash open cabinets in the Commanding Officer's cabin. He then tried some keys which were hanging behind the door and opened a drawer, taking out some confidential books which he gave me. I placed them at the bottom of the hatch. After finding more books in cabinets and drawers I took another lot up."

Brown climbed the ladder and passed the papers to Connell who had rowed over in one of *Petard*'s boats.

Then the teenage Brown said he was going down again. Grazier and Fasson had been trying to free a piece of what looked like radar equipment. But Connell, who had the vantage of rowing in from a distance away, could tell that the U-boat was sinking.

Connell refused to let Brown go back down, instead insisting that he call down the conning tower to the others and tell them to come up immediately.

Ken Lacroix was on the conning tower ladder when he pushed through what felt like a wall of water as waves broke perilously close to the top. Brown was waiting for him.

Lacroix swam away from the U-boat, heading back to the safety of the *Petard*, allowing Brown to call down to the remaining two sailors. Brown remembered that "I saw Grazier, and then the First Lieutenant appeared at the bottom of the hatch. I shouted, 'You had better come up' twice, and they had just started up when the submarine started to sink very quickly."

On the chase boat, Connell watched as the U-boat went down. "The seas were breaking continuously over the remaining portions of the hull that remained visible, the conning-tower, and the water was pouring out through the shell holes. It was a crazy scene. . . . We struggled to hold the sea-boat alongside the conning-tower and at the same time keep afloat. As I was about to jump into the sea and clamber onto the tower, it quite suddenly disappeared, leaving nothing to be seen above the breaking waves. We yelled and called the names of our shipmates. Only Tommy responded, his head bobbing up almost alongside the sea-boat."

After Tommy Brown was pulled into the boat next to an already-rescued Lacroix, Connell asked him, "What about the others?"

"There's no chance," he sputtered. "They were still down below when I dived off."

It was hopeless, yet they called and called, shouting the names of the men who were perishing far below.

The *Petard* hauled the chase boat out of the water while it was still "on the run," searching for the lost shipmates.

FORTY-THREE

KISSES

November and December 1942—Bletchley Park, England

SEVEN MONTHS.

The naval Enigma had been dark for seven months. For all of their genius and inspiration, the codebreakers at Bletchley Park had made no progress.

Commanders at the Admiralty were beyond impatient—they were desperate.

On November 22, 1942, they sent a note to Bletchley Park urging "a little more attention" to the naval Enigma, as if the codebreakers were failing simply from a lack of effort. The U-boat campaign was "the only one in which the war can be lost unless BP do help," came their frantic words.

It wasn't time or effort or intelligence that was lacking; the codebreakers simply couldn't unlock this puzzle by themselves.

Two days after the Admiralty's letter, help arrived.

The codebooks from *U-559*, purchased at the price of Tony Fasson's and Colin Grazier's lives, were finally delivered to Bletchley Park on November 24.

At first, nothing changed. The material from *U-559* did not contain a list of settings for the four-rotor Enigma.

But as the codebreakers pieced through each and every sheet of paper, they found something almost as valuable: a short weather codebook.

In codebreaking, short messages were always safer than long ones; short messages gave fewer chances for an enemy to guess the meaning of words or phrases and form a crib. The Germans knew it, and they knew their weather reports were a weak spot. The reports were sent at the same time, twice a day, every day. It was easy to be predictable, and being predictable was death to any code.

So, to cover their weakness, the Germans made their weather reports as short as possible. Only seven letters long.

Using the short weather codebook, each weather condition was first assigned a letter (for example, 0°C = d) and then reported in a predetermined order: boat latitude, boat longitude, atmospheric pressure, temperature, wind conditions, cloud cover, and visibility.

— 14 —

Tafel 11.

T   T = Lufttemperatur in ganzen Celsius-Graden.

+ 28°¹) C = a	+ 15° C = n	+ 3° C = a	— 10° C = n
+ 27° = b	+ 14° = o	+ 2° = b	— 11° = o
+ 26° = c	+ 13° = p	+ 1° = c	— 12° = p
+ 25° = d	+ 12° = q	0° = d	— 13° = q
+ 24° = e	+ 11° = r	— 1° = e	— 14° = r
+ 23° = f	+ 10° = s	— 2° = f	— 15° = s
+ 22° = g	+ 9° = t	— 3° = g	— 16° = t
+ 21° = h	+ 8° = u	— 4° = h	— 17° = u
+ 20° = i	+ 7° = v	— 5° = i	— 18° = v
+ 19° = j	+ 6° = w	— 6° = j	— 19° = w
+ 18° = k	+ 5° = y	— 7° = k	— 20° = y
+ 17° = l	+ 4° = z	— 8° = l	— 21°²) = z
+ 16° = m		— 9° = m	

Temperatur wegen Schadens am Meßgerät nicht meßbar: x

¹) oder mehr.   ²) oder weniger.

Anmerkung: Bis 0,4° nach unten, von 0,5° an nach oben abrunden.

Beispiele: Abgelesene Temperatur + 7,4° = + 7° = v
              »   »   + 7,5° = + 8° = u

Example table from a short weather codebook.
[www.kartengruppe.it via Wikimedia Commons]

A message that always began "the weather today is" would have been easy to use as a crib. Seven letters that didn't even spell out a word were no help at all.

That is, unless you had the short weather codebook.

And now the codebreakers at Bletchley Park did.

The codebreakers paired the reports from the weather ships with the weather reports broadcast to the general German navy. When the two nets—one from the weather ships and one to the broader navy—created a crib, the codebreakers gave it a special name: they said that the messages "kissed."

There was still the problem of how long it took, even with a perfect kiss, for a bombe to analyze a four-rotor Enigma. But Shaun Wylie solved that on December 13, 1942.

Wylie was one of Turing's friends, recruited from Princeton University, and he realized that the four-rotor weather ships sent messages to land stations, which received messages with a three-rotor Enigma. All of those weather reports had to have been sent with the fourth rotor in a position that forced the machine to act like a three-rotor version. The codebreakers knew how to easily and quickly solve three-rotor versions; all that remained was to find the position of the fourth rotor that allowed it to act as if it wasn't there—the dummy position.

On the Sunday morning that Wylie thought of this idea, he assembled the kisses, created a menu, and then went off to the Bletchley Park canteen to have breakfast while the bombes set to work.

Suddenly, while Wylie was in the middle of his meal, somebody rushed in shouting, "It's out!"

Wylie bolted from the room. He ran back to Hut 8 and then over to Hut 6, shouting, "It's come out in the zero position!"

They had the dummy position—the setting that would make the four-rotor Enigma act like a three-rotor version. It was a discovery so monumental that the wall of secrecy between the two huts was temporarily broken.

Immediately, the codebreakers sat down to begin constructing menus for the bombes. Within minutes, the machines were spinning and clicking away, building up the keys to the naval Enigma that had been dark for seven months.

Hours later, the first broken Shark intercept came through to the Admiralty's Submarine Tracking Room. It revealed the exact location of fifteen U-boats. By the end of December 1942, they were able to place all eighty-four U-boats deployed in the North Atlantic.

Wylie had figured out the dummy position, and the codebreakers had their method of kissing cribs to decipher the naval Enigma. Neither could have been done without the codebooks from *U-559*. Fasson and Grazier had not died in vain.

The two sailors were posthumously awarded Britain's second-highest decoration for bravery, the George Cross. Seven months after the short weather codebooks were delivered to Bletchley Park, King George VI himself awarded Ken Lacroix a decoration for his bravery.

"I know all about it," the king said, referring to the codebooks as he greeted Lacroix. "But we're still not allowed to discuss this, are we?"

"No, it's still a secret," Lacroix responded.

"Well, congratulations," said the king.

And he shook Lacroix's hand.

There was still work to do. It was an art, making kisses from

ADMIRALTY

16th September 1943

MADAM,

I AM COMMANDED BY MY LORDS COMMISSIONERS
OF THE ADMIRALTY TO INFORM YOU THAT, ON THE ADVICE
OF THE FIRST LORD, THE KING HAS BEEN GRACIOUSLY
PLEASED TO APPROVE THE POSTHUMOUS AWARD OF THE
GEORGE CROSS TO YOUR HUSBAND, ABLE SEAMAN COLIN
GRAZIER, FOR HIS OUTSTANDING BRAVERY AND
STEADFAST DEVOTION TO DUTY IN THE FACE OF GREAT
DANGER, WHILE SERVING IN HMS PETARD, IN A MOST
SKILFUL AND SUCCESSFUL HUNT OF AN ENEMY SUBMARINE
IN MEDITERRANEAN WATERS.

I AM EXPRESS THEIR LORDSHIPS' PLEASURE
AT THIS MARK OF HIS MAJESTY'S HIGH APPRECIATION,
AND THEIR DEEP REGRET THAT YOUR HUSBAND DID NOT
LIVE TO RECEIVE IT.

I AM MADAM

YOUR OBEDIENT SERVANT

E.V.MARKHAM.

MRS. OLIVE M. GRAZIER
211 TAMWORTH ROAD,
KINGSBURY,
TAMWORTH.
STAFFS.

Letter from the Admiralty to Colin Grazier's widow on his award of the George Cross.
[Stephencdickson via Wikimedia Commons]

the weather reports, and it didn't always work. At the end of 1942 and in early 1943, there were still blank days, weeks even, where they couldn't quite get a handle on the right pairing, and nothing came out. But it was the beginning of victory, and the codebreakers knew it.

Not only had they discovered a way to read four-rotor Enigma messages, but the number and speed of the bombes quickly multiplied. In fact, when the Germans created new bigram tables again in March, Hugh Alexander remembered that it presented only the smallest of hurdles.

"Now however there were 70 bombes we had no difficulty at all in building up the new bigram tables—to our relief these were not pinched so we had the satisfaction of completing them unaided. . . . It was a fascinating business."

Alexander's relief was clear, the stress and dejection of the blackout replaced by pleasure at the excitement of a game he expected to win.

Yet while the codebreakers at Bletchley Park settled down to unmask and unravel the German intelligence, on the Continent, the Nazis were closing in.

FORTY-FOUR

A FAMILY NAME

June 1941—Paris, France

THE NAZIS WERE still searching for a traitor. Twelve months after Hitler had personally commanded him to find the source of the intelligence leak, Admiral Wilhelm Canaris was empty-handed.

In June, Canaris arrived in Paris, determined to make progress. Lieutenant Colonel Joachim Rohleder had a list of suspects. He had combed through the departments where there had been a link to the leaks. There were only a dozen or so men who had access to the information or were connected to men who possessed those secrets.

At the very top of the list, Rohleder had written *Rodolphe Lemoine*.

Canaris wasn't surprised. The Abwehr had so many files on him that "we would need a wheelbarrow to transport it!" remembered one German officer.

To Canaris, however, the more unexpected name came halfway down Rohleder's list.

"Hans-Thilo Schmidt," Rohleder read.

"Really now . . . you're just looking for a scandal!" Canaris said, throwing his arms up in exasperation. He knew that name—Hans-Thilo was the brother of one of Hitler's leading generals. "You'd dare throw aspersions on one of the largest families of the Reich and one of the most valued leaders of our army? Trust me, abandon that lead."

By the end of the meeting, the Germans had narrowed down their list of suspects to ten men. Hans-Thilo Schmidt was not one of them.

Secretly, though, Rohleder did not agree with Canaris. From that day on, Rohleder made sure that Schmidt was always being watched.

January 9, 1942—unoccupied southern France

Różycki was dead.

He had gone to Africa to help French intelligence decrypt messages there and had been returning to France, traveling in a boat across the Mediterranean Sea. They hit bad winter storms and capsized near the Balearic Islands on January 9, 1942.

He hadn't seen his wife and son since fleeing Poland two and a half years earlier.

The Polish triumvirate of codebreakers was down to two.

FORTY-FIVE

THE FALL OF CADIX

November 6, 1942—France

A DARK BLUE Chevrolet pickup truck and a black Citroën drove slowly toward Château des Fouzes. Bertrand's latest command center, code-named Cadix, was in the southern, unoccupied section of France, only thirty miles north of the coast.

It was barely sunrise when the two vehicles approached. A circular antenna shining in the rising sun clearly marked the truck for what it was: a search vehicle, looking for radio and intercept stations.

Inside the château, the *thud-thud* of Langer's running steps echoed down the hallway.

"Patron! [Boss!]" Langer cried as he pounded on the bathroom door, behind which Bertrand was taking his morning bath. "The Montpellists [French police] are here. As soon as I saw them in the distance, I turned off the radio, but they're coming!"

Doors slammed, even as he spoke. Windows were shut, equipment was stashed away, and, most importantly, all electronics were turned off. Everyone was inside, silent.

"We waited," Bertrand wrote, "watching the horizon from behind the lathes [sic] of the shutters more dead than alive."

The policemen stopped in front of the gate to the château. Three men, all dressed in blue, got out of the Citroën. Every one of them carried a truncheon.

Inside the château, the men barely breathed. If it came to it, Bertrand would go out alone.

The policemen passed the château's gate, walking to the farm next door. It was impossible to hear what was said. But the codebreakers could see. They watched as first one set of neighbors were beaten and then, after a bit of discussion with the farmers on the other side of the château, the second set were beaten as well.

Then, without a backward glance, the police got into their car, and both vehicles drove away.

They would certainly return.

The Nazis had been searching for Bertrand's safe house for more than a month. Day and night, they shut off the region's electrical power at random, unpredictable times, all in an attempt to locate the radio transmitter the codebreakers had built.

Even before the police came to their gate, Bertrand knew it was time to evacuate.

He had returned to the château from arranging evacuation plans only two days before the police arrived. Cadix was barely 150 miles from the line demarcating free and occupied France. Nazi Schnelltruppen (rapid troops) could cover that distance in mere hours.

When Bertrand had arrived back at Cadix, the codebreakers there had handed him a message, transmitted in his own personal code.

"The harvest is good," the message read.

It was a prearranged signal: the Allies were about to invade North Africa, which was territory held by Vichy French forces, who were aligned with the Nazis. As soon as the Allies attacked, the Germans would undoubtedly begin to march south from Paris to the coast. Cadix stood directly in their path.

Immediately, Bertrand made plans to go to Paris. He needed more information. When would the Nazis attack? What was their intended path to the coast? Was it still safe to follow the evacuation route they had drawn up?

Instead, another message came, again enciphered for his eyes only.

"The harvest is very good and there is no time for traveling."

The Allied invasion was imminent. Bertrand had thought he would have a week to prepare. He was wrong.

Example of "safe conduct" passport used in unoccupied France. This example is for passage to Algeria.
[Wikimedia Commons]

The Montpellists returned three more times. They appeared again near Cadix at 1 P.M., 10 P.M., and again the next day, November 7, at 5 A.M., coming very close to, but never directly approaching, Bertrand's hideout. They entered every other building in the neighborhood.

That afternoon, Bertrand got instructions from his supervisor: proceed with the evacuation and advance toward the coast.

The Allies landed in North Africa on November 8, and Cadix was empty by the next morning.

Early in the morning of the 12th, Germans entered the château.

FORTY-SIX

JADWIGA'S STRENGTH
1942—Warsaw, Poland

THERE WAS MORE than one way to find the Polish codebreakers. If they had slipped by the German troops and the French police, then perhaps their whereabouts could be obtained using other methods.

Jadwiga Palluth, wife to Polish electronics wizard Antoni, had remained in Warsaw, in the same house with halls large enough for a young boy to learn to ride a bike and a front entrance that had once hidden illicit radio equipment.

She received a letter, summoning her to the Gestapo headquarters in Warsaw.

It was not a request. It was a command.

Jadwiga went to the massive stone building at 25 Aleja Szucha. Four pairs of stone columns rose three stories tall, bracketing the entrance like the jail bars that held so many people prisoner inside.

There was no ease or informality with the Germans confronting her this time. No mention of tea, herbal or otherwise. The interrogation officer was direct.

"You still say you do not know where your husband is," he charged. "It is very simple. You have two options. Either you tell me, or I will shoot you and the children. You have two minutes to decide which it is."

The building used for the Gestapo headquarters in
Warsaw, Poland, as it stood in the 21ˢᵗ century.
[Najuan via Wikimedia Commons]

Jadwiga, standing straight and tall, looked him directly in the eyes. She answered him immediately.

"Listen to me, Herr Oberst. I am the mother of two boys. As a mother, I choose the option to tell you where he is. But as I do not know where he is, I choose the option that you shoot us."

The Gestapo officer sat, momentarily stunned. He had never confronted someone who chose the "shoot us" option before.

Perhaps, the officer guessed, there was truth in what she said. Perhaps she truly did not know where her husband was. But even if she didn't know Antoni's location right at that moment, perhaps she would lead the Nazis to her husband yet.

Jadwiga was released.

She had received occasional letters from Antoni. It was possible, though neither fast nor easy nor cheap, to get letters through. They never said much, but they let Jadwiga know her husband was alive.

After her visit to the Gestapo headquarters, Antoni's letters continued to come. Now, though, there was a pink line slashed through each message. The Nazis no longer hid that they were reading her mail and any messages—visible or invisible—that might be written in them.

FORTY-SEVEN

FOUND

Winter 1942/1943—France

THE POLISH AND French codebreakers regrouped on the Côte d'Azur in the southeast of France after their flight from Cadix. Bertrand and Langer, now leaders of the French and Polish code-breakers, were left without connections, without means, and without an escape.

A black market of smugglers had begun to flourish, escorting people across the French border to Spain. These smugglers professed no allegiance aside from money. Their services went to the highest bidder, with some even going as far as to sell a client to the Nazis, if the price was right.

Yet after weeks of increasingly desperate messages sent back and forth to London, Bertrand was left with no other option. He and Langer agreed: the Polish cryptographers would rely on smugglers to escape France and eventually make their way to England.

On the evening of January 27, 1943, Rejewski and Zygalski arrived at the train station in Ax-les-Thermes, scant miles from the Spanish border.

The train stopped, and when they walked onto the platform, "two young women threw their arms around our necks and kissed us as if we were good friends," Rejewski remembered.

The two Polish codebreakers had never met these women before, and there was no joy in the introduction. It was a deception, and a necessary one, on the long, fraught path to escape. It wasn't a question whether Germans were watching; the Polish men knew their every move was being observed. These women acted like they were greeting friends, as if Rejewski and Zygalski would be staying and visiting with them, as if the men had no plans of crossing the border or fleeing the country.

But that, of course, was exactly what they intended to do.

Rejewski and Zygalski contacted their smuggler and set a date and time for their departure. They would travel once more by train and then cross the Pyrenees Mountains on foot.

The smuggler had "promised that he would board the train together with us," Rejewski remembered. "Maybe he did, but in any case he did not enter our compartment."

Alone on the train, without any guide, Rejewski and Zygalski decided to press on. When they got off at Latour-de-Carol, they hid in some underbrush, a prearranged backup meeting point.

The smuggler "found us at dusk," wrote Rejewski. "He said he had missed the train. More likely, he hadn't wanted to travel in the same compartment with us for fear of the unpleasant consequences if we fell into the hands of the Germans."

They went to a tavern, ate some supper, and attempted a few quick hours of sleep.

Then, with darkness as their only cover, Rejewski and Zygalski started for the Spanish border on the night of January 29, 1943. The smuggler guided them through the area surrounding the train station, managing to avoid both the Nazi and French patrols.

As they were going, they burned their French identification

papers and any documents connecting them with France. If the Spanish patrols caught them, it would be better to be jailed in Spain than to get sent back to France to face internment at the nearby Le Vernet concentration camp.

Over the rocky and then snowy passes of the Pyrenees, they crept past the last French villages and houses.

It was after midnight when the smuggler began muttering to himself.

In broken French, the smuggler raised his voice to shouting. He hadn't been paid! He hadn't seen a single franc, and this was dangerous, he cursed! Suddenly, he pulled out a gun.

The men might have been mere steps from Spain, but Rejewski and Zygalski were lost, entirely dependent on their guide. In the cold night, they were nothing without the man who was now fiddling with the trigger of his pistol.

So they paid him.

A few hours later, Rejewski and Zygalski crossed the border. Out of the range of the Nazis, they now faced new threats. Heavily armed Spanish security forces combed the area for refugees crossing illegally. Very few foreigners made it through the border towns without being picked up.

Just before daybreak on January 30—mere hours after they had begun their flight from Latour-de-Carol—Rejewski and Zygalski were arrested.

The two Polish codebreakers spent the next three and a half months in crowded Spanish jails. It couldn't be compared to the horrors of the Nazi concentration camps, but thousands of prisoners were crammed into single-room facilities like sports arenas, given little food, and subjected to beatings and harassment.

Conditions didn't change much until the prisoners in one such Spanish jail instituted a hunger strike. After three days, the frailest of the prisoners began to collapse, and the Spanish authorities started to panic. If the prisoners died, it might draw Allied attention. They would do anything to avoid that scrutiny and the power behind it. The Spanish government agreed to begin letting the prisoners go free.

Rejewski and Zygalski walked out of prison on May 4 and reached Madrid, the Spanish capital, on May 19.

They were the lucky ones.

Spring 1943—France

By March 10, Langer, Ciężki, and Palluth had tried to cross the French-Spanish border twice. The first time, the appropriate officials had not been bribed in advance, and the men spent a month in a French jail. The second time, they suspected that their smuggler, a man named Gomez, actually tipped off the Gestapo to their presence. Luckily, they escaped without notice.

Their third trip began differently. The three men, along with one additional Polish refugee, planned to cross the border with an agent named Perez, who both included the men in his planning and agreed to personally escort them to Spain.

To guarantee their safety, Bertrand—who was staying behind to work with the French Resistance—said he would only pay the smuggler after the men were safely in Spain. So, before they left, Perez had Langer sign a twenty-franc note, which the smuggler then ripped in half, giving one piece to Bertrand and one piece to Langer. The plan was that after crossing the border, Langer would return his half to Perez, and then Perez would present Langer's signed half to Bertrand. The two matching pieces together would be proof that Perez had completed his job, and then Bertrand could pay him what was owed. It seemed like a fair arrangement.

But the night of their departure, nothing went as planned. Perez backed out at the last moment, saying that Gomez would now be their guide. Two Frenchmen looking to flee the country were also added, increasing the size of the group to six men plus the guide. Still, the Polish codebreakers, anxious to be out of France, agreed to go ahead with the escape.

All six men hid in the back of a French police car, which Gomez had bribed some official to "borrow." They drove to Elne, a small border town, where a second guide was to help them cross the Pyrenees on foot. At the handoff between guides, Langer relinquished his half of the signed twenty-franc note.

"About three kilometers out of Elne, out of a grove of young trees there suddenly jumped out military . . . Gestapo men, and almost simultaneously others drove up on motorcycles from behind and in front. They began firing, surrounded us, and arrested us, letting the guide go free," remembered Langer. "Next they drove us . . . to the Gestapo [for] the first interrogation."

For the next two years, Langer and Ciężki were placed in Stalag 122 in Compiègne as prisoners of war and then Schloss Eisenberg internment camp in Czechoslovakia. Palluth was taken to the Sachsenhausen-Oranienburg concentration camp in Germany.

It was never determined how Langer's true identity, rather than the alias he gave them, was discovered. But almost a year after his arrest, Langer was pulled aside again.

"I was expecting the worst," he remembered. "I was sat down in front of a panel. . . . They were all wearing plain clothes. The Gestapo officer spoke first: 'You were in the intelligence service,' he said."

It was a statement, not a question. They knew.

Would Langer work for them, the Nazis wondered. They had others, they said, who had turned.

"At that point I interrupted, and said that you can only die once."

Langer would never help them, even if they threatened to kill him.

"After that, [the Nazi interrogator] did not persist," Langer remembered, but instead said, "Oh I see."

The Nazis, however, were not finished. If Langer wouldn't work for them, then they wanted to know about the work he *had* done, back in Poland.

"When he asked me, without looking me in the eye, if we had read any machine ciphers during the war," Langer remembered, "I realized he must know something about what had happened."

"I decided that I had to use the following strategy, given that I was dealing with experts, who knew who I was. I mixed truth with lies, and tried to present my lies in such a way that they had the veneer of truth."

Half-truths would always be more convincing than whole lies.

"When answering this, I made sure that I did not harm anyone, nor did my answer do any damage to our cause," Langer remembered. "I told him that before the war, we conducted tests, and sometimes we did find a solution, but during the war, we didn't manage to decode anything, since the Germans had made changes, which they knew about, just before the war started."

"Since I was dealing with experts," Langer continued, "and since Major Cięzki knew more about the subject than I did, it was better that I did not try to go into the details in case there was a conflict."

His interrogators called Cięzki into the room. Somehow, Cięzki picked up on Langer's story. He agreed: the Polish codebreakers had broken Enigma before the war, and then changes to the procedure had once again put them in the dark.

It was the truth—*a* truth—though certainly not the whole truth.

But it was enough.

Their story worked, "because although [the officers] were supposed to see us again, they never came," wrote Langer.

Back in France, back in the spring of 1943, Bertrand knew nothing of what was to become of Langer, Ciężki, and Palluth.

When Perez handed over Langer's half of the twenty-franc note on March 12, 1943, Bertrand paid him the agreed-upon six hundred thousand francs in full. There were other things on his mind.

The Abwehr had found Lemoine.

FORTY-EIGHT

I WAS EXPECTING YOU TOMORROW

Winter 1942 to spring 1943—France

LEMOINE HAD CONNECTIONS everywhere. That was his job: to know people who knew things and to get them to tell him what they knew. He was very good at it.

On December 10, 1942, he received a message from contacts in Marseille that the Germans were coming for him and his wife.

Unfortunately, that was not the only message he received.

As Lemoine and his wife rushed about, preparing to escape to Spain, the phone rang. It was a call from their son. He had been arrested.

"He was speaking in such a way," Lemoine's wife recalled, "that I could tell a Gestapo agent was standing right next to him."

Lemoine and his wife changed plans. Rather than escaping themselves, they decided to stay in France, to do what they could for their son.

It was all a setup, a ploy to get Lemoine to stay put. Quickly, an old acquaintance going by the name Hubertus, now working for the Germans, managed to make contact with Lemoine once again.

"I allowed myself to confide in him, which then motivated him to do likewise," Hubertus remembered. "A few days later, we had become old friends talking openly about the situation. . . ."

Through their conversations, it became obvious to Hubertus that Lemoine felt no special loyalty to the Allied cause. In fact, as an anti-Communist, Lemoine's feelings now seemed rather aligned with Germany, who was at war with the Communist USSR, one of the Allies, fighting with the US and England.

"I hate and despise the English as much as it is possible to imagine," explained Lemoine, "and if the [French] marshal gave me orders to fight against the English and to rally on the side of the Germans, I would do so with all my heart and with great pleasure."

He went even further one day, saying that "it is lamentable that the pernicious Anglo-Saxon [British] propaganda blinds the world about the terrible danger which makes it run from the horrifying threat of communism that Germany alone is currently fighting. It is necessary that Germany wins the war, for if not, it is the end for all of Europe and its civilization."

Lemoine appeared so strongly anti-English and anti-Communist that Hubertus was certain Lemoine would collaborate with the Nazis, given the proper inducement to do so. In the report to his Nazi handlers, Hubertus concluded that, considering Lemoine's "connections around the world and his potential, it would be most useful to rally his services which I believe he is entirely prepared to offer us."

After he read the report, Admiral Wilhelm Canaris, chief of the Abwehr, gave clear instructions: "Sequester Lemoine and his wife immediately. Treat them with respect, and keep the matter in absolute secrecy."

On February 27, 1943, at 4:30 P.M., Captain George Wiegand of the Abwehr approached Lemoine's house in Saillagouse. Lemoine was in the middle of a conversation with Hubertus, unaware that anything was about to happen.

It was one of the few times in his life that Lemoine was surprised.

"I was expecting you tomorrow," said the best-connected man in France, astonished at his slip in timing.

It was hardly an arrest, and certainly not one with any speed or immediate unfortunate consequences. Wiegand took his time, going so far as to help Lemoine organize his bills and set his affairs in order. When Wiegand came across Lemoine's bank account, he left the entire sum intact. Only when Lemoine and his wife were ready did the Nazi agent finally escort them back to Paris.

Wiegand noted that on the way, "Lemoine spoke to me about his activities with the Deuxième Bureau. He told me that he would be willing to tell me everything and be of assistance."

March 1943—Paris, France

In Paris, the Abwehr officers reiterated Canaris's orders: "Lemoine has been brought back to Paris not as a prisoner but as guest of honor. There can be no question of arrest."

He and his wife were installed at the Hotel Continental, one of the very places where Lemoine used to shower money and luxury on friends and recruits.

Lemoine spared himself no indulgence. He and his wife lived luxuriously in apartment 159. An attendant brought the couple their food and could acquire anything they needed, even if it meant buying it on the black market.

But this was not peacetime. And Lemoine was not on vacation. His interrogation began on March 2.

He began by attempting to justify himself: "I can no longer position myself against Germany as a loyal Frenchman and Anglophobe. So I am going to place myself at the disposal of the German authority."

The first to be given up was one of the people closest to him: a man who was his accomplice during his time in the unoccupied territory of France.

"Believe me," Lemoine explained, "if I talk about him right now it's because he's working for our English enemies. This German Jew is a Communist. He has a hatred of his homeland. . . . You will find [him] at the home of his mistress."

Hubertus himself was dispatched to recover this first of Lemoine's reveals. It took him four months, and a promise of ten thousand francs, but Hubertus discovered the man on July 14. Two days later, the man was found dead in his prison cell, from suicide or murder, no one knew or cared to discover.

But what the Germans really wanted was the name of the spy inside their own ranks. First they tried to persuade Lemoine to reveal his source. Then they tried threatening him with all the power of the Abwehr. Finally, they went for his weakest point: money.

Lemoine had used money—the promise of it, the luxury, the cool comfort it brought—to lure so many of his assets to speak. In the end, he could not resist the temptation himself.

In exchange for a huge sum, he spilled the whole story, from Hans Thilo-Schmidt's first disheveled, almost begging appearance in Verviers, Belgium, to his delivery of intelligence and Enigma documents over the course of many years. It took three days for Lemoine to explain it all.

Near the end of his story, Lemoine attempted to justify himself once more: "[Schmidt's] greed and venality are such that having severed all contact with us since 1939, I fear that he has sought out new resources by working for the Soviets."

It was a claim Lemoine made without any supporting evidence. Even if true, though it likely was not, it changed nothing.

Lemoine had just betrayed his greatest asset.

Hans-Thilo Schmidt was easy to find. Had the Abwehr not already been following him, his name and address were listed in the phone book.

He had known this day was coming. If it hadn't been Lemoine, it would have been someone else and sometime soon.

Schmidt had long ago started looking over his shoulder when he was on the street. It was almost certain his phone was tapped and his letters read.

One day, anxious and despairing, he slipped a few cyanide pills into his inner belt, which he never took off.

They came for him at 6 A.M. on March 22, 1943—less than a week after Lemoine gave him up.

FORTY-NINE

SCHMIDT

Spring to summer 1943—Berlin, Germany

THEY FOUND HIM, and they arrested him. What to do next with Hans-Thilo Schmidt, a.k.a. Asché, was a more complicated question.

It would not do to expose the depth of the leak with a long trial or public sentence. Yet Schmidt could not be allowed to go unpunished—what kind of message would that send to others who might be considering treason?

For the spring and summer of 1943, the German traitor and lover of money was held in a prison near Berlin. Schmidt's daughter, Gisela, was the only one allowed in to see him.

She had been the first one in the family to discover he had been arrested. The Gestapo would tell the Schmidt family nothing: neither the charges against him nor the name of the prison where he was being held. It wasn't until Gisela encountered a family friend at Gestapo headquarters that she made any progress in her search. And even then, she was told that going to see her father would throw her under suspicion as well.

She went anyway.

Her father was noticeably thinner, but otherwise apparently

unharmed. Guards watched their every move and listened to their every word. Rather than say anything that could possibly incriminate her father, Gisela had written him a note, saying she loved him no matter what. He silently mouthed back, "Be brave, my darling, be brave."

At the end of the visit, he asked her to take his heavy winter coat and bring back his lighter one. Then, seizing upon a moment when the guards weren't looking, he urgently whispered, "Cut the arm off the coat. There's something inside for you."

It was a note, asking her to sew cyanide pills into the lining of the lighter coat he had asked her to bring to the prison.

Gisela was familiar with suicide. Both her brother and her mother had already attempted it since her father's arrest. In both cases, Gisela was the one to find and rescue them.

Now, rather than prevent a death, she contacted her high school chemistry professor, who was known to have Jewish ancestors and therefore was likely to act against the Nazis. He gave her the pills and assured her they were indeed strong enough.

But Gisela was not allowed back into the prison. Instead, she gave the coat to the Gestapo family friend.

Later, the same friend warned her that the pills had been found and to never try a trick like that again.

That summer, her brother also attempted to do as his father had asked. The same chemistry teacher gave cyanide pills to him, too, and, somehow, he got them to his father. Perhaps, by that point, the Nazis realized that Schmidt's suicide would be the fastest way to end their embarrassment over the Enigma treason; after Gisela's attempt, they might have changed their mind and been willing to turn a blind eye. Or perhaps Gisela's brother used a more clandestine method. She never found out.

Schmidt was buried in an unmarked grave outside of Berlin on September 21, 1943.

Gisela had been called to the prison to collect her father's body, and she had looked and saw that it was unharmed. There had been no other torture besides what his own mind had done to itself.

His treason was considered so volatile that no one outside of his and Lemoine's interrogators and a few people within Hitler's inner circle were told what he had done.

But it was too late for the Nazis to preserve their secret. Enigma had already been broken.

FIFTY

BERTRAND

Summer 1943—Gulf of Cadiz, Portugal

AFTER ALL THEY had been through, the final steps to England were almost easy. Marian Rejewski and Henryk Zygalski crossed the border from Spain to Portugal without incident before heading south to the Gulf of Cadiz.

One night, they left the fishing village where they had been staying, traveling out onto the gulf in a small boat. At the exact time and in the exact place that had been agreed upon, British ships took form out of the blackness and a sailor threw a narrow, swaying gangplank down to the codebreakers.

"Go on—jump!" he shouted, waving the men across the water.

The two Polish cryptographers—who had broken ciphers in Poland, France, Africa, and unoccupied French territory; who had witnessed the attacks on Warsaw and the bombing of Paris; who had spent three months in squalid Spanish prisons—arrived at the British territory of Gibraltar on July 24, 1943. Less than two weeks later, they flew to England.

Upon their arrival, they were exempted from the usual interrogation procedure, which sought to weed out Nazi infiltration into the country. Someone high-ranking had decided that they knew too much and could not even be questioned by British counterintelligence.

Yet the British government never entirely trusted the Polish men. When Bertrand had heard that Rejewski and Zygalski were headed for England, he had exclaimed, "Quelle aubaine pour les Anglais!" [What a windfall for the English!] But it was a treasure never realized. The very geniuses who had first broken Enigma spent the rest of the war decrypting other signals. They never worked on Enigma again.

By the end of the summer of 1943, the whole of the Enigma group from Warsaw and Paris had either been arrested or had escaped.

All except for one. Bertrand.

Winter 1944—Paris, France

Bertrand was finished with Enigma. He had done what he could to see its secrets unlocked and Hitler's army crushed as a result.

Bertrand moved on to other Resistance activities, and on January 3, 1944, he left for his 101st mission: to pick up some radio equipment from an agent in Paris.

Sacré-Coeur rose majestic, high above the bustling streets of Montmartre, Paris. Inside, stained-glass windows and tall, imposing statues lined the walls of the famous cathedral.

There had been a plan— there was always a plan; the risk was never in the plan, but

Sacré-Coeur, Paris.
[Tonchino via Wikimedia Commons]

in the slight tremors of the unknown that made a thousand little decisions sum to destiny.

The man was to be carrying a copy of *Signals* magazine. He should arrive between 9 and 9:30 A.M. They would meet in front of the statue of Saint Anthony of Padua, the tall, robed figure holding a small child, the infant Jesus. When Bertrand greeted him, saying, "Salve," the man should respond, "Amen."

Bertrand arrived early. At 9:20 A.M., a man arrived and knelt down in reverence to Saint Anthony.

But there was no copy of the magazine. And when Bertrand said, "Salve," the man only beckoned him forward.

Bertrand followed him anyway.

The man said he had only been able to decode half of the message Bertrand had sent to relay their plan for this meeting.

Perhaps, Bertrand thought, the agreed-upon codeword and the magazine had been lost in the other half of the message. He continued with the meeting.

Bertrand wanted equipment, and the man said he could get it all. The man wrote down the time and place of their next meeting in a small red notebook.

Agents of the Resistance did not write down appointments. They memorized them.

And yet, as they had agreed, Bertrand set out to meet the man once again on the morning of January 5, fighting the feeling that something was wrong.

At eight o'clock, the time they had agreed, the man did not appear. Instead, Bertrand watched from behind a pillar as three strangers walked to the statue of Saint Anthony.

A fourth man rushed to them and almost immediately rushed out again.

Bertrand was just about to leave when he felt a hand on his shoulder. A man's voice told him that it would be better for him if he remained still.

Bertrand was under arrest.

Monsieur Masuay was exactly the man you would picture to torture victims into submission: depressed, dour-looking, and morbidly dressed in a scarlet shirt and black tie.

Bertrand was not a fool. It only took the mention of torture, and he realized he would tell them everything—one way or another. The first truth to come out was his real name.

It was at that point, on finding out Bertrand's real name, that everything changed. Bertrand had been carrying false papers, of course, and the Nazis had realized he was working under an alias. But they hadn't realized just how monumental a prize they had captured. The Nazis had assumed they'd caught a courier for the Resistance; they had instead found the mastermind of the French intelligence agency.

Bertrand was taken to the Hotel Continental and placed in a comfortable suite, not unlike the one given to Lemoine and his wife. There, plied with offers to obtain anything he liked, the questioning took a much different turn.

"Everything can still get better," said the next man who came to question Bertrand.

Perhaps it was a reflection on the previous conversations with Lemoine, perhaps it was simply a ploy to try to find a unifying goal, but the Nazi interrogator then spent a long time lecturing about the threat of Communism.

At the end, he finally spoke the offer that Bertrand had expected: "You should help the country in its fight against the common enemy," the Nazi said. "Would you be willing to cooperate loyally with us? It would be understood that you would be asked to do nothing against your country. . . . Your expertise would assist us with the double radio game with the British, who are your worst enemies."

Bertrand knew the implied choice: help us or talk—by force, if necessary. The Nazis had not yet connected him to Enigma, which they believed to still be secure. The choice to switch sides might not be given again once they found out.

"Okay," replied Bertrand. Agreeing with that single word to become a double agent.

"But I must be free," he continued. "Nothing should arouse suspicion on the part of my friends with whom I have meetings in Vichy."

The Nazis agreed. Bertrand was given freedom of movement in exchange for promised intelligence.

One week later, he slipped away from the Abwehr agents tailing him. Bertrand had escaped.

The official notice was posted on January 28:

Cdt. B. ist sofort nach Ankunft in Clermont-Ferrand geflohen—hat Ehrenwort gebrochen. [Commander Bertrand has fled immediately after his arrival in Clermont-Ferrand—he failed to keep his word of honor.]

Honor, to Bertrand, held a deeper meaning. He never performed a single act of treachery against the Resistance and never gave the Nazis a single piece of information against the Allied cause. He was, however, able to pass on valuable information about Nazi interrogation to his contacts in the French Resistance.

"Rely on my total dedication right to the end—even in playing hide-and-seek with the Gestapo," Bertrand had written to a friend nearly a year earlier. He was true to his word.

It took another four months to arrange his evacuation, but Bertrand and his wife were flown with a third member of the Resistance, a Jesuit priest, to England on June 2, 1944.

That night, a curious radio message was broadcast by the British Broadcasting Corporation (BBC) from London. It simply said, "Michel has shaved off his moustache."

The Allied and Resistance agents listening in across the English Channel knew it meant that Bertrand had arrived safely.

Paul Paillole, who had led the Deuxième Bureau before the German invasion and had helped form the Travaux Ruraux organization secretly in occupied France, had made his way to London several months before. When Bertrand arrived, Paillole officially interviewed his friend for the British government for two days, both talking freely about their escapes and what had gone on since they fled Cadix.

"The spontaneous, unrestrained joy that Bertrand displayed as soon as he saw me was shocking," Paillole wrote. "His look was sharp, blunt, familiar, like old times. . . . He answered my questions, happy to tell his story. My beliefs were confirmed: the Abwehr had been masterfully played."

Bertrand was safe.

And so was the Enigma secret.

EPILOGUE

BY THE LATTER days of the war, Hugh Alexander could report that naval Enigma messages "reached Admiralty on an average 30 minutes after the time of intercept. The record was 19 minutes." More than 84,000 messages were read each month because of keys broken by the bombes, coming to about two Enigma messages read every minute.

The information gathered from reading decrypted Enigma messages helped the Allies win on many fronts. In the Battle of the Atlantic, Enigma messages showed the locations of individual U-boats in near real time. In North Africa, Enigma intelligence described troop movements and the plans of the German general Erwin Rommel, which directly led to his defeat.

Later, when the Allies were planning their massive assault on the European continent, an operation known as D-Day, they also laid false plans to trick the Germans into believing a different time and location of attack. Enigma communications showed that the Germans were convinced of these decoy plans. Then, when the real D-Day invasion began, intercepted and decrypted Enigma messages first alerted the Allies that they had been seen by the enemy.

Decades later, Harry Hinsley would calculate that reading Enigma messages shortened the war by three years, undoubtedly preventing untold numbers from perishing on the battlefields and in concentration camps.

Time and again, the Nazis had within their grasp the people and information to understand that Enigma had been broken. Lemoine and Hans-Thilo Schmidt could have told their interrogators that the machines had been reproduced. Langer, Ciężki, and Bertrand, had they been pushed even a little, might have broken and told every detail of their technical accomplishments, both on the Continent and in Britain.

Yet the Nazis' confidence was their ultimate weakness. As Paul Paillole concluded years after the war, "as ludicrous as it may seem today, the Germans never seriously accepted that the Allies could break their codes using scientific methods."

Breaking the naval Enigma was a testament to teamwork. There was not one hero, not even one team of heroes. The Enigma story played out over the course of more than a decade, with action spread throughout almost a dozen countries: Polish cryptologists worked early and long to first crack the Enigma cipher; French and German spies and agents provided intelligence; British codebreakers took up the puzzle; naval ships and sailors seized codebooks from the U-boats; intercept stations relayed messages; and Wrens at the bombes actually ran the machines.

"The Hut 8 cryptologists," Alexander wrote, "sitting down on their own with messages in front of them and trying to get it out by genius would have got nothing but a headache."

Many of the major figures in this story—codebreakers and spies alike—lived through the war, though few would ever tell the tale of working to break Enigma's secrets.

THE POLISH TEAM

MARIAN REJEWSKI, one of the original trio of Polish codebreakers, returned to Poland, to his wife, kids, and eventual grandkids. Though he was never given a position in Communist Poland equal to his mathematical genius, he managed to live comfortably before dying in 1980. He lived long enough for the Enigma secret to come to light and gave many interviews and lectures, and wrote several reports about his work in the last years before his death.

HENRYK ZYGALSKI, the other member of the Polish code-breaking trio to survive the war, remained in England, becoming a lecturer at Battersea Polytechnic (which later became the University of Surrey). He received an honorary doctorate for his work in 1977 and died the next year, 1978.

GWIDO LANGER, the head of the Polish cipher office at the outbreak of the war, was freed from the concentration camp where he was held prisoner and moved to England. Tragically, some of the officers in the Polish military, both those trapped in France and those waiting in England, blamed him for not arranging for the codebreakers to escape to London earlier. He died in 1948 without being recognized for his heroism in helping break Enigma.

MAKSYMILIAN CIĘŻKI, who led the German-language section of the Polish cipher office before the invasion of Poland, followed a similar, unfortunate path. Blamed for not enabling an earlier escape, he, too, died in 1951 before his courage could be brought to light.

ANTONI PALLUTH, the Polish electronics genius who first built a reproduction of the Enigma machine in Warsaw, was captured while trying to cross into Spain along with Langer and Ciężki. He was imprisoned in the Sachsenhausen-Oranienburg concentration camp near Berlin and died from Allied bombs while he was working as a slave laborer in a German factory on April 18, 1944. He continued to write coded letters to his wife, Jadwiga, until his death. The Germans never realized that the Palluth they had arrested and placed in a concentration camp was the same man from Warsaw they had sought throughout the war.

JADWIGA PALLUTH, who repeatedly stood up to Nazi interrogation in order to keep the Enigma secret safe, remained active in the Polish resistance until the Germans were defeated. She survived the terror of Nazi-occupied Warsaw, though the big house where her son had learned to ride his bike and she had hidden radio equipment directly in front of Nazi eyes was entirely destroyed. She left the ruined city after the war, first working at a ski resort and then as a seamstress to provide for her sons until she died of liver cancer in 1952.

THE BRITISH TEAM

ALAN TURING, mastermind of the English cryptological bombe, left Hut 8 in the fall of 1942 to work for GC&CS in the United States and did not return to the Enigma project at Bletchley Park for the rest of the war. Hugh Alexander would later write that "there should be no question in anyone's mind that Turing's work was the biggest factor in Hut 8's success. In the early days he was the only cryptographer who thought the problem worth tackling. . . . It is always difficult to say that anyone is absolutely indispensable but if anyone was indispensable to Hut 8 it was Turing." After the war, back home in England, he worked on developing the first computers. He was prosecuted in 1952 for being gay, which was a crime in England at the time. As an alternative to prison, he agreed to undergo female hormone treatment that was designed to reduce or eliminate sexual desire. Two years later, he was found dead in his apartment from cyanide poisoning.

GORDON WELCHMAN, who devised the spider bombe's diagonal board and led Hut 6 at Bletchley Park, moved to the United States after the war and worked for decades in the defense industry.

In 1982, he wrote a book about the Enigma effort at Bletchley Park, *The Hut Six Story*. Many people believed that the details of breaking Enigma should still have been kept secret, and Welchman lost his security clearance and position in the defense industry as a result. He died, never having cleared his name, in 1985.

HARRY HINSLEY, who developed traffic analysis for Enigma messages and first suggested seizing codebooks from weather ships, was only twenty-six when the war ended. He went back to St. John's College, Cambridge, where he became a history professor and authored the definitive, five-volume tome on British Intelligence during the Second World War. He died in 1998.

HUGH ALEXANDER, one of the original four "wicked uncles" of Bletchley Park, continued to work in cryptography for the British government until his retirement in 1971. An avid, accomplished chess player, he went on to write several books about the game while also authoring an unpublished, yet still widely available and often cited, text about the breaking of the naval Enigma at Bletchley Park, which was only declassified in 1999. He died in 1974.

JOAN CLARKE (later **JOAN MURRAY**), who proved that Banburismus worked in practice as well as theory, continued to work for the British government in communications headquarters until her retirement in 1977. She became a renowned authority on several types of old coins before assisting Harry Hinsley with one of his volumes on wartime intelligence. She died in 1996.

THE FRENCH TEAM

GUSTAVE BERTRAND, the intelligence agent who first brought Hans-Thilo Schmidt's documents to the Polish cryptographers, continued working for the French Secret Service for a few years after the war before becoming a politician and eventually the mayor of Théoule-sur-Mer in southern France. He wrote the first account of the French efforts to break Enigma, describing the help they received from Hans-Thilo Schmidt, in his book *Enigma, ou la Plus Grande Énigme de la Guerre, 1939–1945* [*Enigma, or the Greatest Enigma of the War, 1939–1945*], published in 1973. He died in 1976.

PAUL PAILLOLE, who was head of the Deuxième Bureau and later led French counterespionage through Travaux Ruraux, left civil service immediately after the war to work in industry. Decades later, he wrote two books, one of which detailed Hans-Thilo Schmidt's story, his contributions to the French Intelligence, and Lemoine's eventual betrayal of Asché. He died in 2002.

RODOLPHE LEMOINE, the agent to first meet with—and ultimately betray—Hans-Thilo Schmidt, was captured and questioned by French authorities when the Allies invaded France. He died of natural causes, while still under investigation, in 1946.

THE GERMANS

KARL DÖNITZ, admiral of the German U-boat fleet, was made successor to Hitler in the latter's last will, completed only days before his suicide. To Dönitz's surprise, and the surprise of nearly everyone else as well, he became the German head of state on May 2, 1945. He was tried for war crimes during the Nuremberg Trials and sentenced to ten years in prison. Though his Laconia Order suspending any rescue at sea could have merited the death penalty, it was decided not to pursue this sentence because Admiral Chester Nimitz of the United States had authorized "unrestricted warfare" (including no rescue of survivors) against the Japanese as well. Dönitz died in 1980 in West Germany.

WILHELM CANARIS, who led the search for a leak within Hitler's inner circle, was the chief of the German military intelligence service, the Abwehr, until February 1944. However, during the war, he had been leading a double life and was heavily involved in the anti-Hitler movement. He was arrested by German authorities and executed on April 9, 1945, after helping to organize an attempt on Hitler's life.

Breaking Enigma was a wartime effort that helped the Allies to win the war, but, since then, the art of keeping secrets has only grown.

Today, cryptology touches virtually everyone. By text messaging, sending emails, or shopping online, you send your information through ciphers many times more complex than Enigma.

More than ever in today's digital world, these codes are built on complex math instead of language patterns. Bletchley Park is now a museum rather than an operational center for intelligence, but geniuses the world over are still working to develop more intricate puzzles and veils to keep the world secure—to keep the world safe.

TIMELINE

1929

JANUARY—a German Enigma machine is discovered in the Polish customs office and examined by Antoni Palluth along with two others.

- Palluth and Maksymilian Ciężki begin traveling to Poznań University to teach a course on cryptology. Three of their most promising students are Marian Rejewski, Henryk Zygalski, and Jerzy Różycki.

1931

NOVEMBER 1—Hans-Thilo Schmidt meets with Rodolphe Lemoine for the first time. One week later, he begins regularly passing Lemoine and Gustave Bertrand highly classified German secrets.

DECEMBER—Bertrand visits Warsaw, Poland, and hands the first of Schmidt's materials to Gwido Langer.

1932

NOVEMBER—Rejewski begins working on the Enigma problem.

1933

JANUARY—Rejewski breaks the Enigma cipher for the first time, "as by magic."

JANUARY 30—Adolf Hitler becomes chancellor of Germany.

1938

MARCH 9—Lemoine is arrested by the Gestapo and taken to Berlin for questioning.

MARCH 12—Nazi troops cross the German-Austrian border.

SEPTEMBER—Hitler annexes the Sudetenland area of Czechoslovakia.

OCTOBER—Using patterns in each message's indicator settings, Rejewski formulates plans for the Polish bomba machine. At about the same time, Zygalski invents the eponymous Zygalski sheets as another method of discovering the Enigma settings.

DECEMBER 15—Germans add two more Enigma rotors to the available catalogue, bringing the total number to five. As a result, the Polish codebreakers are no longer able to read Enigma messages.

1939

JANUARY 9 AND 10—Codebreakers from Britain, France, and Poland meet in Paris. Not much information is exchanged, but relationships develop, and a code—"there is something new"—is set in place to call another meeting.

JULY 24—British, French, and Polish codebreakers meet again, this time in Warsaw, where the Polish codebreakers reveal that they broke Enigma and read messages for several years before the messages became indecipherable seven months earlier.

AUGUST 31—Harry Hinsley barely escapes to France from Germany before borders are closed.

SEPTEMBER 1—Germany invades Poland.

SEPTEMBER 3—England and France declare war on Germany.

SEPTEMBER 6—The Polish cryptographers flee Warsaw for temporary safety in Romania.

1940

JANUARY—Alan Turing visits the Polish and French codebreakers at PC Bruno and in Paris.

FEBRUARY 12—HMS *Gleaner* sinks *U-33*, and Enigma rotors are captured.

MARCH 1—Turing's first bombe, Victory, is installed at Bletchley Park.

MARCH 10—Hans-Thilo Schmidt/Asché meets with an agent of the Deuxième Bureau for the last time.

APRIL 26—HMS *Griffin* captures the German patrol boat *Schiff 26*, which has been disguised as *Polares*. Gunner Florrie Foord dives into the water to retrieve a duffel bag full of codebooks.

MAY—Three days of German naval Enigma messages are broken on Victory using the cribs provided by *Schiff 26/Polares*. Without pinches to supply a complete set of bigram tables or further supply cribs, no more naval Enigma messages can be read.

- Harry Hinsley uses traffic analysis to deduce that Nazi ships are being rerouted from the Mediterranean Sea to the northern Atlantic near Norway. He cannot convince anyone at the Admiralty of his information, and several British ships are sunk in June as a result.

- Herivel Tips begin to be used to regularly break the German army/air force Enigma net.

MAY 10—German troops begin the invasion of Luxembourg, Belgium, and the Netherlands.

MAY 31—*U-13* is sunk off the coast of Lowestoft, England, spurring

Dönitz to doubt the security of Enigma. No changes to the cipher or operations are made.

JUNE—German forces begin bombing Paris on June 3. Bertrand moves the Polish codebreakers to southern France and then, quickly, to Algeria.

JUNE 16—Hitler personally orders a search for the leak of information, which will lead to Lemoine's and Schmidt's eventual arrests.

LATE JUNE—Lemoine refuses evacuation to England.

AUGUST—The second British bombe, and the first to be built with Welchman's diagonal board, is installed at Bletchley Park.

• German Admiral Karl Dönitz begins his U-boat "wolfpack" strategy.

SEPTEMBER 12—Ian Fleming (eventual author of the James Bond novels) presents plans for Operation Ruthless. Unfortunately, no German ships are spotted when his plans are put into action, and no codebooks are obtained.

NOVEMBER—Using the spider bombe and Banburismus, the codebreakers at Bletchley Park read another three days of German naval Enigma messages. The startling messages from June 26 inform them that all-new bigram tables came into effect on July 1. The codebreakers have no hope of reading messages intercepted after that date without stealing new codebooks.

1941

MARCH 4—*Krebs*, a German trawler, is captured off the coast of Norway. From the information pinched from her seizure, the codebreakers are able to reconstruct the bigram tables and use Banburismus to identify which rotors are being used.

MAY 7—At Harry Hinsley's suggestion, a German weather ship,

München, is captured, providing all the naval Enigma settings for June 1941.

MAY 9—*U-110* is captured, providing the Offizier settings for Enigma, the method by which naval officers communicate with one another.

JUNE 28—*Lauenburg*, another weather ship, is captured. Information taken from the seizure allows the Bletchley Park cryptologists to reconstruct new bigram tables.

SEPTEMBER 6—Prime Minister Winston Churchill visits Bletchley Park.

OCTOBER 21—The four "wicked uncles" of Bletchley Park (Gordon Welchman, Alan Turing, Hugh Alexander, and Stuart Milner-Barry) write to Churchill, explaining that Enigma decryption and intelligence work is suffering due to lack of resources. He responds immediately with an Action This Day memo.

1942

JANUARY 9—Różycki dies while crossing the Mediterranean Sea from Africa on his way back to France.

FEBRUARY 1—The Shark U-boat net begins using four rotors in their Enigma machines. The naval Enigma net at Bletchley Park goes dark once again.

AUGUST—Three hundred U-boats, the number that Dönitz has long said is needed for German victory, are at the disposal of the German navy for the first time.

SEPTEMBER 17—Dönitz issues his Laconia Order, which forbids U-boats from rescuing any survivors of their attacks.

OCTOBER 30—*U-559* is captured by HMS *Petard*. Two British seamen drown while seizing German codebooks.

DECEMBER 13—Bletchley Park codebreakers break German naval Enigma once more using information from *U-559*.

1943

JANUARY 29—Rejewski and Zygalski cross the border from France to Spain and are immediately arrested.

FEBRUARY 27—Lemoine is arrested. Though he is taken to Paris as a "guest" of the Abwehr, he faces months of interrogation.

MARCH 10—Langer, Ciężki, and Palluth are betrayed by the guide hired to smuggle them from France into Spain, and are arrested by the Gestapo. They will spend the next two years in concentration camps.

MARCH 22—Hans-Thilo Schmidt/Asché is arrested in Berlin.

MAY—Rejewski and Zygalski are released from Spanish prison on May 4 and arrive in Madrid on May 19. From there, they make their way to a small fishing village in Portugal.

JULY 24—Rejewski and Zygalski arrive on British-controlled Gibraltar.

SEPTEMBER 21—Hans-Thilo Schmidt is buried in an unmarked grave outside of Berlin after having died by suicide.

1944

JANUARY 5—Bertrand is arrested during a mission for the French Resistance.

JANUARY 28—After having agreed to work as a double agent for the Nazis, Bertrand slips away and goes into hiding.

JUNE 2—Bertrand arrives safely in London.

JUNE 6—Allied troops land in Normandy, France, beginning the D-Day invasion that will lead to the end of World War II in Europe.

ACKNOWLEDGMENTS

RESEARCHING IS ALWAYS an interesting process. Researching during a pandemic is an adventure. The first, heartfelt thank you for this book—the only reason I could write this book while the world struggled under the weight of COVID-19—is due to librarians. I'm particularly grateful to the wonderful people at the Washington-Centerville Public Library and the Cincinnati and Hamilton County libraries. You make a difference and are truly appreciated.

I am greatly indebted to people near and far who willingly shared their knowledge of cryptography and their experiences with Enigma. Dermot Turing not only provided an invaluable resource in his book *X, Y & Z: The Real Story of How Enigma Was Broken*, but he very generously shared images and put me in touch with sources. Beata Majchrowska helped me get to know the stories of Antoni and Jadwiga Palluth—heroes, both!—and, with the patience of a saint, coached me in the pronunciation of Polish names. Additional thanks is due to Paul Reuvers, Szymon Dabrowski, Rosie Burke, and Joel Greenberg.

Julia and Elliot McCurdy—danke! (Which is about as far as I can get without your help! Thank you both!)

Critique partners see more flaws than anyone, yet they somehow still offer the encouragement to go on. I'm thankful for the friendship and wisdom of Rebecca Morris, Tracy Vonder Brink, Andrew Speno, and Danielle Frimenko.

To my agent, Michael Bourret; editor, Brian Geffen; and the

team at Holt—thank you! Michael, I'm so grateful for the potential you can see in the merest of ideas. Brian, I am blown away by your insight and vision. Our conversations regularly leave me so energized that I often have to go for a run before I can sit down to write! Thank you for taking on this project and coaching it through to the end. I'm also grateful for the efforts of Sarah Kaufman, Aurora Parlagreco, Lelia Mander, Ana Deboo, Edmund Mander, Samira Iravani, Shane Rebenschied, Kelsey Marrujo, Carina Licon, Jie Yang, Jaime Herbeck, and Veronica Ambrose in turning a text into this gorgeous book.

Mom, Dad, Nika, Hilary, and Katya, any love of words I have is due entirely to the best of times with all of you. Because of you, I laugh every time I read a monograph (or, for that matter, meet anyone under a table). Love you!

Dominic, Adam, and Lydia—always.

BIBLIOGRAPHY

6812th Signal Security Detachment. *The US 6812 Bombe Report 1944*. Translated by Tony Sale, 15 June 1945, codesandciphers.org.uk/documents/bmbrpt/usbmbrpt.pdf.

Alexander, C. H. O'D. *Cryptographic History of Work on the German Naval Enigma*. Accessed November 9, 2020, ellsbury.com/gne/gne-000.htm.

America's National Churchill Museum. "Winston Churchill: Gathering Storm." Accessed December 19, 2020, nationalchurchillmuseum.org/winston-churchill-and-the-gathering -storm.html.

Baker, Joanne. "Forgotten Heroes of the Enigma Story." *Nature*, vol. 561 (September 2018): pp. 307–08 or doi.org/10.1038/d41586-018-06149-y.

Bamford, Tyler. "Nazi Germany's Last Leader: Admiral Karl Dönitz." The National WWII Museum, New Orleans, June 11, 2020. nationalww2museum.org/war/articles/nazi-germanys -leader-admiral-karl-donitz.

Batey, Mavis. *Dilly: The Man Who Broke Enigmas*. Biteback Publishing, 2009.

BBC. "Breaking Germany's Enigma Code." Accessed September 10, 2020, bbc.co.uk/history/ worldwars/wwtwo/enigma_01.shtml.

Beesly, Patrick, et al. *Ultra and the Battle of the Atlantic*. 1977, nsa.gov/Portals/70/documents/ news-features/declassified-documents/cryptologic-spectrum/Ultra.pdf.

Blaney, Debi. "*U-576*: Life and Death on a World War II German U-Boat." NOAA Ocean Exploration and Research, September 4, 2016, oceanexplorer.noaa.gov/explorations/ 16battlefield/logs/sept4/sept4.html.

Bletchley Park. "Roll of Honour—Norman Allon Bacon." Bletchley Park. Accessed September 12, 2020, rollofhonour.bletchleypark.org.uk/roll-of-honour/325.

Budiansky, Stephen. *Battle of Wits: The Complete Story of Codebreaking in World War II*. The Free Press, 2000.

Burman, Annie. "Gendering Decryption—Decrypting Gender: The Gender Discourse of Labour at Bletchley Park, 1939–1945." Master's thesis, Uppsala University, 2013. uu.diva -portal.org/smash/get/diva2:625771/FULLTEXT01.pdf.

Busch, Harald. *U-Boats at War*. Ballantine Books, 1955.

Carter, Frank. "The Turing Bombe." The Rutherford Journal. Accessed February 5, 2021, rutherfordjournal.org/article030108.html.

Casselman, Bill. "The Polish Attack on Enigma II: Zygalski Sheets." American Mathematical Society. Accessed September 9, 2020, ams.org/publicoutreach/feature-column/fc-2013-12.

Chichester Observer. "Naval Officer Who Helped to Break the Enigma Code." November 30, 2017. chichester.co.uk/news/naval-officer-who-helped-break-enigma-code-1066980.

Churchill, Winston. *Their Finest Hour.* RosettaBooks, 2002.

———. "Churchill's Action This Day Memo on Supply of Labour for Bletchley Park." The National Archives. images.nationalarchives.gov.uk/assetbank-nationalarchives/action/viewAsset?id=47277&index=261&total=396&view=viewSearchItem.

Clark, Lloyd. *The Battle of the Tanks: Kursk, 1943.* Open Road + Grove/Atlantic, 2011.

"U-boat Operations: U-boat Force Combat Strength." Uboat.Net. Accessed February 15, 2021, uboat.net/ops/combat_strength.html.

Copeland, B. J. "Ultra: Allied Intelligence Project." *Encyclopedia Britannica.* Accessed January 28, 2021, britannica.com/topic/Ultra-Allied-intelligence-project.

Copeland, B. Jack. *Turing: Pioneer of the Information Age.* Oxford University Press, 2012.

Copeland, Jack. "Alan Turing: The Codebreaker Who Saved 'Millions of Lives.'" BBC News, June 19, 2012. bbc.com/news/technology-18419691.

Crypto Museum. "Bigram Tables." Accessed October 7, 2020, cryptomuseum.com/crypto/codebook/bigram.htm.

———. "Enigma G." Accessed October 16, 2020, cryptomuseum.com/crypto/enigma/g/index.htm.

———. "Gordon Welchman: Codebreaker." Accessed April 10, 2021, cryptomuseum.com/people/gordon_welchman.htm.

Davis, Nicola. "How Britain's Second World War Spirit Benefited Science." *The Guardian,* January 18, 2015. theguardian.com/science/2015/jan/18/how-britains-second-world-war-spirit-benefited-science-winston-churchill.

Dimbleby, Jonathan. *The Battle of the Atlantic: How the Allies Won the War.* Oxford University Press, 2016.

Doenitz, Karl. *Memoirs: Ten Years and Twenty Days.* Translated by R. H. Stevens, Da Capo Press, 1997.

Douglas Archives Genealogy Pages. "Sir Marshall George Clitheroe (3rd Bt) Warmington." douglashistory.co.uk/famgen/getperson.php?personID=I76731&tree=tree1.

Encyclopedia Britannica editors. "Mein Kampf: Quotes, Summary, & Analysis." Encyclopedia Britannica. Accessed August 28, 2021, britannica.com/topic/Mein-Kampf.

———. "Wilhelm Canaris: German Admiral." Encyclopedia Britannica. Accessed March 6, 2021. britannica.com/biography/Wilhelm-Canaris.

Eyewitness to History. "The Beginning of World War II, 1939." Published 2004. eyewitnesstohistory.com/ultimatum.htm.

Fitzgerald, Penelope. *The Knox Brothers.* Counterpoint, 2000.

Free Library. "It's Not a Welcome Memory. Two of Our Men Were Killed and I Nearly Died but We Did Capture the Vital Codes: Seizing the Enigma: Sole Survivor Tells of U-Boat Raid."

The Free Library, Accessed February 27, 2021, https://www.thefreelibrary.com/It's+not+a+welcome+memory.+Two+of+our+men+were+killed+and+I+nearly . . . -a062672896

Garliński Józef. *The Enigma War*. Charles Scribner's Sons, 1979.

Gaulle, Charles de. "Charles de Gaulle Speech," BBC News. Last updated June 17, 2010, bbc.co.uk/news/10339678.

Halifax, Lord Edward. "World War Two Ultimatum Letter to Germany." The British Library .bl.uk/collection-items/wwii—ultimatum-letter.

Harvey, Ian. "Predators of the Seas: Life Inside a U-Boat—In 41 Images." War History Online, September 22, 2018, warhistoryonline.com/instant-articles/inside-a-german-u -boat.html.

Hegranes, Emily. "Sinking and Submerged: Emergency Escape Equipment for Submarines." U.S. Naval Institute Naval History Blog, March 26, 2019. navalhistory.org/2019/03/26/ sinking-and-submerged-emergency-escape-equipment-for-submarines.

Hinsley, F. H., E. E. Thomas, et al. *British Intelligence in the Second World War: Volume 1, Its Influence on Strategy and Operations*. Cambridge University Press, 1979.

Hinsley, F. H., E. E. Thomas, et al. *British Intelligence in the Second World War: Volume 2, Its Influence on Strategy and Operations*. Cambridge University Press, 1981.

Hinsley, F. H., et al. *British Intelligence in the Second World War: Volume 3 Part 1, Its Influence on Strategy and Operations*. Cambridge University Press, 1984.

Hinsley, F. H., and Alan Stripp, editors. *Codebreakers: The Inside Story of Bletchley Park*. Oxford University Press, 1993.

Hinsley, Harry. "The Influence of ULTRA in the Second World War." Transcript of seminar held October 19, 1993. www.cix.co.uk/~klockstone/hinsley.htm.

"Historical Currency Conversions" (online calculator). futureboy.us/fsp/dollar.fsp.

History.com editors. "Adolf Hitler Is Named Chancellor of Germany." History.com, October 28, 2009. history.com/this-day-in-history/adolf-hitler-is-named-chancellor-of-germany.

———. "Beer Hall Putsch." History.com. Accessed September 4, 2021, history.com/topics/ germany/beer-hall-putsch.

———. "Germany Invades Poland." History.com, November 16, 2009. history.com/this-day -in-history/germany-invades-poland.

———. "Pearl Harbor Bombed." History.com, November 24, 2009. history.com/this-day-in -history/pearl-harbor-bombed.

Hodges, Andrew. *Alan Turing: The Enigma*. Random House, 2014.

Holocaust Explained, The. "Hitler Becomes Chancellor." Accessed December 8, 2020, theholocaustexplained.org/the-nazi-rise-to-power/the-nazi-rise-to-power/hitler -becomes-chancellor/.

Holwitt, Joel. "Learn from Fleet Boat Development." U.S. Naval Institute, February 2020. usni.org/magazines/naval-history-magazine/2020/february/learn-fleet-boat-development.

Holzer, Frank. "What Made Austria Welcome Hitler." *New York Times*, April 13, 1985. *NYTimes.com*. nytimes.com/1985/04/13/opinion/l-what-made-austria-welcome -hitler-164833.html.

Kahn, David. *Seizing the Enigma: The Race to Break the German U-Boat Codes, 1939–1943.* Houghton Mifflin Co., 1991.

Khan Academy. "The Enigma Encryption Machine." (Video). Accessed July 29, 2020, khanacademy.org/computing/computer-science/cryptography/crypt/v/case-study-ww2 -encryption-machines.

Klein, Christopher. "Chamberlain Declares 'Peace for Our Time.'" History.com, September 30, 2013. history.com/news/chamberlain-declares-peace-for-our-time-75-years-ago.

Körner, T. W. *The Pleasures of Counting*. Cambridge University Press, 1996. Also available at the Internet Archive, archive.org/details/pleasuresofcount0000korn.

Kozaczuk, Władysław. *Enigma: How the German Machine Cipher Was Broken, and How It Was Read by the Allies in World War Two*. Translated by Christopher Kasparek, University Publications of America, 1984.

Kruh, Louis, and Cipher Deavours. "The Commercial Enigma: Beginnings of Machine Cryptography." *Cryptologia*, vol. 26, no. 1 (January 2002): pp. 1–16. www.cryptomuseum .com/crypto/enigma/files/KruhDeavours.pdf.

Lance, Rachel. "How to Escape From a Sunken Submarine." *Wired*, April 4, 2020. wired.com/ story/how-escape-sunken-submarine/.

Last, Nella. *The Diaries of Nella Last: Writing in War and Peace*. Profile Books, 2012.

———. *Nella Last's War: A Mother's Diary, 1939–1945*. Sphere, 1983.

Linehan, Peter. "Obituary: Professor Sir Harry Hinsley." *The Independent*, February 19, 1998. independent.co.uk/news/obituaries/obituary-professor-sir-harry-hinsley-1145675.html.

Local, The. "Hitler Didn't Intend to Annex Austria So Quickly, Then the Joyful Crowds Changed His Mind." March 8, 2018. thelocal.de/20180308/hitler-wehrmacht -annexation-austria.

Lugo, Jack. "Operation Ruthless: Ian Fleming's Plan to Capture Enigma Codebooks." *Artistic Licence Renewed: The Literary James Bond Magazine*, January 10, 2015. literary007 .com/2015/01/10/operation-ruthless-ian-flemings-plan-to-capture-enigma-codebooks/.

Majchrowska, Beata. Interview with Rebecca E. F. Barone. Personal interview. April 9, 2021.

Marcuse, Harold. "Historical Dollar-to-Marks Currency Conversion Page." Accessed April 26, 2021, marcuse.faculty.history.ucsb.edu/projects/currency.htm.

Mawdsley, Evan. "America and WW2: When, How, and Why Did the US Get Involved, and Why They Didn't Enter Sooner?" History Extra. Accessed July 9, 2021, historyextra.com/ period/second-world-war/why-when-how-america-entered-ww2-pearl-harbor-roosevelt/.

McCarthy, Jeremy. "The Enigma of the Polish Bomba." BCS, July 8, 2019. bcs.org/content -hub/the-enigma-of-the-polish-bomba/.

McDougall, Walter A. "20th-Century International Relations—Poland and Soviet Anxiety." *Encyclopedia Britannica*, July 26, 1999. britannica.com/topic/20th-century-international -relations-2085155.

McKay, Sinclair. *The Secret Lives of Codebreakers: The Men and Women Who Cracked the Enigma Code at Bletchley Park*. Penguin, 2012.

Miller, Joe. "Joan Clarke, Woman Who Cracked Enigma Cyphers with Alan Turing." BBC News, November 10, 2014. bbc.com/news/technology-29840653.

Miller, Nathan. *War at Sea: A Naval History of World War II*. Oxford University Press, 1996.

Milner-Barry, Stuart. "Conel Hugh O'Donel Alexander: A Personal Memoir." Declassified document, available at web.archive.org/web/20130918021633/http://www.nsa.gov/ public_info/_files/cryptologic_spectrum/cono_hugh.pdf.

Mortimer, Gavin. "The Battle of the Atlantic: Why Britain Almost Lost to Hitler's U-Boats." History Extra, May 27, 2020. historyextra.com/period/second-world-war/did-britain -almost-lose-battle-atlantic-ww2-athenia-sinking/.

Murray, Joan. "A Personal Contribution to the Bombe Story." *NSA Technical Journal*, vol. 20, no. 4 (1975): pp. 41–46.

Murray, Williamson. "Churchill Takes Charge." HistoryNet, February 13, 2008. historynet .com/churchill-takes-charge.htm.

National Cyberspace Security Center. "Traditions." Narodowe Centrum Bezpiecze stwa Cyberprzestrzeni. Accessed November 13, 2020, https://ncbc.wp.mil.pl/pl/pages/tradycje -2017-01-16-6/.

National Museum of Computing. "The Turing-Welchman Bombe." Accessed October 29, 2020, tnmoc.org/bombe.

National Ocean Service, NOAA. "How Far Does Light Travel in the Ocean?" Accessed September 28, 2020, oceanservice.noaa.gov/facts/light_travel.html.

National Weather Service, NOAA. "Layers of the Ocean." Accessed September 28, 2020, weather.gov/jetstream/layers_ocean.

Naval History and Heritage Command. "Japanese Midget Submarines Used in the Attack on Pearl Harbor." Accessed July 25, 2021, history.navy.mil/our-collections/photography/ wars-and-events/world-war-ii/pearl-harbor-raid/japanese-forces-in-the-pearl-harbor-attack/ japanese-midget-submarines-used-in-the-attack-on-pearl-harbor.html.

New York Times. "Nazis Won First 12 Reichstag Seats in 1928." November 13, 1933, p. 2.

Oord, Christian. "The Hidden Dangers of Serving on a German U-Boat During WW2." War History Online, May 5, 2019. warhistoryonline.com/instant-articles/horrors-of-serving-a-u-boat .html.

Paillole, Paul. *The Spy in Hitler's Inner Circle: Hans-Thilo Schmidt and the Intelligence Network That Decoded Enigma*. Translated by Curtis Key and Hannah McAdams. Casemate, 2016.

Perimeter Institute for Theoretical Physics. *The Inner Workings of an Enigma Machine* (2014). youtube.com/watch?v=mcX7iO_XCFA.

Piotrowski, Tadeusz. *Poland's Holocaust: Ethnic Strife, Collaboration with Occupying Forces and Genocide in the Second Republic, 1918–1947*. McFarland, 2007.

Range, Peter Ross. "How Adolf Hitler Turned a Year in Jail into a Step Toward Power." *Time*, January 26, 2016. time.com/4192760/hitler-munich-excerpt/.

Rising, David. "Hitler's Cushy Prison Life in the 1920s Revealed." *Independent*, June 24, 2010. independent.co.uk/news/world/europe/hitler-s-cushy-prison-life-1920s -revealed-2008754.html.

Roberts, Andrew. *The Storm of War: A New History of the Second World War*. HarperCollins, 2011.

Röll, Hans-Joachim. "The Loss of U 33." Deutsches U-Boot-Museum. Accessed October 14, 2020, http://dubm.de/en/the-loss-uf-u-33/.

Roosevelt, Franklin D. "The President Requests War Declaration 125." Library of Congress. loc.gov/resource/afc1986022.afc1986022_ms2201/?st=text.

Royal Navy. "#OTD Shortly After 11am in 1939" Twitter, September 3, 2019. twitter.com/ RoyalNavy/status/1168805810937503746.

Royde-Smith, John Graham. "World War II, 1939–1945." *Encyclopedia Britannica*. Accessed February 16, 2021, britannica.com/event/World-War-II.

Russell, Thomas Arthur. "Approach of the Storm." BBC—WW2 People's War, November 25, 2005, bbc.co.uk/history/ww2peopleswar/stories/93/a7277493.shtml.

Sale, Tony. "The Breaking of German Naval Enigma: Banburismus." Accessed October 22, 2020, codesandciphers.org.uk/virtualbp/navenigma/navenig4.htm.

———. "Technical Specification of the Enigma: The Enigma Rotors." Accessed December 16, 2020, codesandciphers.org.uk/enigma/rotorspec.htm.

Sebag-Montefiore, Hugh. *Enigma: The Battle for the Code*. Wiley, 2001.

Simkin, John. "Francis Harry Hinsley." Spartacus Educational, January 2020. spartacus -educational.com/Francis_Harry_Hinsley.htm.

———. "Government Code and Cypher School." Spartacus Educational, January 2020, spartacus-educational.com/GCCS.htm.

Steinway, Roger. "Interview: U-Boat Survivor's Story." HistoryNet, March 23, 2020. historynet.com/interview-u-boat-survivors-story.htm.

Stevenson, William. *Spymistress: The Life of Vera Atkins, the Greatest Female Secret Agent of World War II*. Arcade Publishing, 2007.

Stripp, Alan. *How the Enigma Works*. PBS/NOVA, November 9, 1999. pbs.org/wgbh/nova/ article/how-enigma-works/.

Terraine, John. *The U-Boat Wars: 1916–1945*. G. P. Putnam's Sons, 1989.

Turing, Dermot. *X, Y & Z: The Real Story of How Enigma Was Broken*. The History Press Ltd, 2019.

U-Boat Aces. "Life Aboard a U-Boat." Accessed September 28, 2020, uboataces.com/articles -life-uboat.shtml.

Ullrich, Volker. *Hitler: Ascent, 1889–1939.* Alfred A. Knopf, 2016.

United States Holocaust Memorial Museum. "Path to Nazi Genocide Worksheet: Answer Key." Accessed August 28, 2021, ushmm.org/m/pdfs/USHMM-Path-Worksheet-Answer -Key.pdf.

Venosa, Ali. "Breaking Point: How Much Water Pressure Can the Human Body Take?" *Medical Daily*, August 13, 2015. medicaldaily.com/breaking-point-how-much-water-pressure-can -human-body-take-347570.

Veterans Affairs Canada. "The Battle of the Atlantic." Date modified: January 27, 2020. veterans .gc.ca/eng/remembrance/history/historical-sheets/atlantic.

Welchman, Gordon. *The Hut Six Story: Breaking the Enigma Codes.* McGraw-Hill Book Company, 1982.

Wilcox, Jennifer. *Solving the Enigma: History of the Cryptanalytic Bombe.* National Security Agency, 2006. nsa.gov/Portals/70/documents/about/cryptologic-heritage/historical -figures-publications/publications/wwii/solving_enigma.pdf.

Williams, Andrew. *The Battle of the Atlantic: Hitler's Gray Wolves of the Sea and the Allies' Desperate Struggle to Defeat Them.* Basic Books, 2003.

Williamson, Samuel H. "Purchasing Power Today of a US Dollar Transaction in the Past." MeasuringWorth.com. measuringworth.com/calculators/ppowerus/.

Winder, Davey. "The Rarest of WWII Nazi Enigma Encryption Machines Just Sold for $440,000." *Forbes*, July 21, 2020. forbes.com/sites/daveywinder/2020/07/21 /the-rarest-of-wwii-nazi-enigma-encryption-machines-just-sold-for-440000-christies -auction-technology/#2e0dcf761fe8.

Winterbotham, F. W. *The Ultra Secret.* Harper & Row, 1974.

WorthPoint. "German U Boat Escape Emergency Breathing Apparatus WWII Kriegsmarine Submarine." Accessed July 2, 2021, worthpoint.com/worthopedia/german-boat-escape -emergency-1814020577.

Wright, John. "The Turing Bombe Victory and the First Naval Enigma Decrypts." *Cryptologia*, vol. 41, no. 4 (2017). tandfonline.com/doi/abs/10.1080/01611194.2016.1219786.

ENDNOTES

AUTHOR'S NOTE

"Deciphering is . . . decoding": Hugh Alexander, *Cryptographic History of Work on the German Naval Enigma*, 87.

CHAPTER 1

"You are expected . . . 12 noon": Paul Paillole, *The Spy in Hitler's Inner Circle: Hans-Thilo Schmidt and the Intelligence Network That Decoded Enigma*, 9.

"Guten Morgen . . . I represent the French Intelligence Bureau": Paillole, *The Spy in Hitler's Inner Circle*, 10–11.

"an amazing person . . . charm of the man": Paillole, *The Spy in Hitler's Inner Circle*, 18.

"You must have . . . another glass of whiskey": Paillole, *The Spy in Hitler's Inner Circle*, 11.

"I've been desperate . . . on Sunday": Paillole, *The Spy in Hitler's Inner Circle*, 12–13.

"settled in . . . in suite 31": Paillole, *The Spy in Hitler's Inner Circle*, 22.

"We apologize . . . a few documents": Paillole, *The Spy in Hitler's Inner Circle*, 23.

"but my chief . . . dare not ask for it": Paillole, *The Spy in Hitler's Inner Circle*, 23.

"He will . . . back to Berlin": Paillole, *The Spy in Hitler's Inner Circle*, 23.

"the thread . . . heart of the Enigma mystery": Paillole, *The Spy in Hitler's Inner Circle*, 24.

"Mechanical encryption . . . time on it": Paillole, *The Spy in Hitler's Inner Circle*, 24.

CHAPTER 2

"The only ones . . . are the Poles": Paillole, *The Spy in Hitler's Inner Circle*, 21.

"an explosion of amazement and joy": Paillole, *The Spy in Hitler's Inner Circle*, 25.

"This is extraordinary and unexpected": Paillole, *The Spy in Hitler's Inner Circle*, 26.

"They were radiant": Paillole, *The Spy in Hitler's Inner Circle*, 26.

"The Schmidt documents . . . in the desert": Dermot Turing, *X, Y & Z: The Real Story of How Enigma Was Broken*, 66.

"Vous avez fait . . . our gratitude": Turing, *X, Y & Z*, 66.

"You do not have the same motivations . . . save years of work": Paillole, *The Spy in Hitler's Inner Circle*, 26.

CHAPTER 3

"the Germans reasoned . . . read any message": Władysław Kozaczuk, *Enigma*, 250.

CHAPTER 4

"In the long report . . . truly shock you": Paillole, *The Spy in Hitler's Inner Circle*, 45.

"It is simple . . . starch solution": Paillole, *The Spy in Hitler's Inner Circle*, 14.

"an incredible tangle . . . exits in another": Paillole, *The Spy in Hitler's Inner Circle*, 28.

"Your route is impeccable, but it's so long": Paillole, *The Spy in Hitler's Inner Circle*, 29.

"At this rate . . . informants put together": Paillole, *The Spy in Hitler's Inner Circle*, 29.

CHAPTER 5

"All who are not of a good race . . . bloody process": "Mein Kampf," *Britannica*, britannica.com/topic/Mein-Kampf.

"Either the enemy . . . we over theirs": Peter Ross Range, "How Adolf Hitler Turned a Year in Jail into a Step Toward Power," *Time.com*, January 26, 2016, time.com/4192760/hitler-munich-excerpt/.

CHAPTER 6

"seek information . . . strictly confidential work": Turing, *X, Y & Z*, 44.

"Maybe it's a year? . . . Friedrich der Grosse geboren": Kozaczuk, *Enigma*, 10–11.

CHAPTER 7

"Mr. Rejewski, do you have any spare time . . . what you are working on": Turing, *X, Y & Z*, 69–70.

"In a staff, and particularly in a cipher bureau, it's not customary to ask questions": Kozaczuk, *Enigma*, 232.

"I was . . . abandoned by my predecessors": Kozaczuk, *Enigma*, 251.

"With normal algebra . . . back where you started": Turing, *X, Y & Z*, 70.

"Mr. Rejewski . . . any of your colleagues, though": Turing, *X, Y & Z*, 70–71.

"quite unexpectedly . . . October 1932": Kozaczuk, *Enigma*, 256.

"that is how the matter . . . they weren't": Kozaczuk, *Enigma*, 257.

"This time . . . from my pencil, as by magic": Kozaczuk, *Enigma*, 258.

"a man like me . . . cannot yield": Volker Ullrich, *Hitler: Ascent, 1889–1939*, 329.

"The history of Hitler is the history of people underestimating him": Ullrich, *Hitler*, 378.

CHAPTER 8

"We had the impression . . . had happened": Kozaczuk, *Enigma*, 43.

"My beautiful mother . . . proud of me": Hugh Sebag-Montefiore, *Enigma*, 26.

"clock room": Kozaczuk, *Enigma*, 234.

"Everything was in concrete bunkers . . . night in silence": Kozaczuk, *Enigma*, 46.

"a very popular . . . eating it": Kozaczuk, *Enigma*, 63.

"could calculate . . . entire cipher key": Kozaczuk, *Enigma,* 289.

CHAPTER 9

"languages, false names . . . record for larceny": Turing, *X, Y & Z*, 54.

"What did you give them? . . . keep or not keep": Paillole, *The Spy in Hitler's Inner Circle*, 113.

"I know from Asché . . . all contact with Asché": Paillole, *The Spy in Hitler's Inner Circle*, 113–114.

CHAPTER 10

"Any resistance is to be broken mercilessly": Kozaczuk, *Enigma*, 45.

"As Führer . . . the German empire": "Hitler Didn't Intend to Annex Austria So Quickly, Then the Joyful Crowds Changed His Mind," *The Local DE*, March 8, 2018, www.thelocal .de/20180308/hitler-wehrmacht-annexation-austria

"What [will come] . . . [what will follow] the explosion": Kozaczuk, *Enigma*, 46.

"My good friends . . . peace for our time": Christopher Klein, "Chamberlain Declares 'Peace for Our Time,'" History.com, September 20, 2013, history.com/news/chamberlain -declares-peace-for-our-time-75-years-ago

CHAPTER 11

"quickly found the connections . . . finding the keys": Kozaczuk, *Enigma*, 63.

CHAPTER 12

"#29 . . . concerning the Enigma cipher machine (Navy model)": Turing, *X, Y & Z*, 90.

"of very great interest . . . of very considerable value to us": Turing, *X, Y & Z*, 90.

"They were indeed completely in the dark": Paillole, *The Spy in Hitler's Inner Circle*, 240.

"Dear Colonel . . . and in war": Turing, *X, Y & Z*, 92.

"to convince our enemy . . . Enigma had been read": Paillole, *The Spy in Hitler's Inner Circle*, 140.

"the Poles begged us not to do anything": Paillole, *The Spy in Hitler's Inner Circle*, 140.

"which were even more clumsy than mine": Turing, *X, Y & Z*, 114.

"*The Poles* . . . enigma nil": Turing, *X, Y & Z*, 114.

"from a technical perspective, it was disappointing": Paillole, *The Spy in Hitler's Inner Circle*, 141.

"no light was shed . . . born out of it": Paillole, *The Spy in Hitler's Inner Circle*, 240.

"There is something new": Kozaczuk, *Enigma*, 56.

CHAPTER 13

"I'll cook them in a stew they'll choke on": Walter A. McDougall, "20th-Century International Relations—Poland and Soviet Anxiety," *Britannica*, July 26, 1999, www.britannica.com/topic/ 20th-century-international-relations-2085155/Poland-and-Soviet-anxiety.

"is unlikely": Andrew Roberts, *The Storm of War*, 9.

"The decision remains . . . There will be fighting": Lloyd Clark, *The Battle of the Tanks: Kursk, 1943*, 26.

"Il y a du nouveau": Kozaczuk, *Enigma*, 67.

"ate and drank too much": Mavis Batey, *Dilly: The Man Who Broke Enigmas*, 74.

"to see Germany . . . before all hell broke loose": Batey, *Dilly*, 74.

"froid, nerveux, ascète": Batey, *Dilly*, 74.

"stony silence . . . about something": Turing, *X, Y & Z*, 121.

"He suddenly let himself go . . . or pinched it": Batey, *Dilly*, 75.

"Where did you get . . . built by our cryptanalysts": Józef Garliński, *The Enigma War*, 43.

"Quel est le QWERTZU": Batey, *Dilly*, 76.

"Nous avons . . . ensemble": Batey, *Dilly*, 77.

"I am fairly clear . . . capable and honest": Batey, *Dilly*, 76.

"If I understand correctly . . . going on in Warsaw": Paillole, *The Spy in Hitler's Inner Circle*, 144.

"I was sure that . . . regained his pride": Paul Paillole, *The Spy in Hitler's Inner Circle,* 144.

CHAPTER 14

"Get him . . . at the latest": Sebag-Montefiore, *Enigma*, 43.

CHAPTER 15

"The object of war . . . Polish descent or language": Tadeusz Piotrowski, *Poland's Holocaust: Ethnic Strife, Collaboration with Occupying Forces and Genocide in the Second Republic, 1918–1947,* 117.

"Burning of papers . . . evening, departure": Kozaczuk, *Enigma*, 77.

"Outside Mińsk, a stop in the woods": Kozaczuk, *Enigma*, 77.

"Air raids and bombings . . . burning Siedlce": Kozaczuk, *Enigma*, 77.

"stuffed beyond any normal capacity": Kozaczuk, *Enigma*, 79.

"Befehl ist Befehl . . . we did": Kozaczuk, *Enigma*, 79.

"Come back . . . a rebuff": Kozaczuk, *Enigma*, 79.

"Please just tell your superior that we are friends of Bolek": Kozaczuk, *Enigma*, 73.

"Mais oui . . . speaking with Paris": Kozaczuk, *Enigma*, 73.

"Ah, you have no passports . . . That's no problem": Kozaczuk, *Enigma*, 79.

"besieged [by] thousands of people . . . who wanted to get passports, too": Kozaczuk, *Enigma*, 79.

"they immediately gave us passports . . . [and] they stamped them": Kozaczuk, *Enigma*, 79.

"You will watch . . . most treasured possessions": Turing, *X, Y & Z*, 136–137.

"Young, in good health . . . Extraordinary": Kozaczuk, *Enigma*, 74.

CHAPTER 16

"TOTAL GERMANY. Repeat. TOTAL GERMANY": Royal Navy [@RoyalNavy], September 3, 2019, "#OTD shortly after 11 A.M. in 1939, the Admiralty sent the uncoded signal to all warships, establishments, and merchant shipping: TOTAL GERMANY. Repeat. TOTAL GERMANY. Britain was at war. #WW2 #threadtweet #80years https://t.co/Vq0hCNSn2U"

"sat immobile, gazing before him": Eyewitness to History, "The Beginning of World War II, 1939," 2004, www.eyewitnesstohistory.com/ultimatum.htm

"Mein Gott! . . . war with England again": John Terraine, *The U-Boat Wars: 1916–1945*, 215.

"We know our enemy . . . we will win": Terraine, *The U-Boat Wars*, 215.

"we really did not think . . . a desperate one": Andrew Williams, *The Battle of the Atlantic: Hitler's Gray Wolves of the Sea and the Allies' Desperate Struggle to Defeat Them*, 2.

"finis Germaniae": Nathan Miller, *War at Sea: A Naval History of World War II*, 34

"He had enormous charisma . . . captivated by this charisma": Williams, *The Battle of the Atlantic*, 22.

"I was fascinated . . . part of the whole": Jonathan Dimbleby, *The Battle of the Atlantic: How the Allies Won the War*, 18.

"On board . . . devil out of hell": Debi Blaney, "*U-576*: Life and Death on a World War II German U-Boat," NOAA Ocean Exploration and Research, September 4, 2016, https://oceanexplorer.noaa.gov/explorations/16battlefield/logs/sept4/sept4.html

"very big ships with very big guns": Williams, *The Battle of the Atlantic*, 26.

"I wanted to imbue . . . would not suffice": Karl Doenitz, *Memoirs: Ten Years and Twenty Days*, 13.

"How safe was the code? . . . But the jackpot exists": Williams, *The Battle of the Atlantic*, 130.

CHAPTER 17

"At first in France . . . out of the question": Kozaczuk, *Enigma*, 94.

CHAPTER 18

"That's very good . . . on my harpsichord": Sebag-Montefiore, *Enigma*, 43.

"It was all done with minimum fuss and maximum dispatch": F. H. Hinsley and Alan Stripp, *Codebreakers: The Inside Story of Bletchley Park*, 77.

"I'm going there too": Sebag-Montefiore, *Enigma*, 44.

"nightmare," "hideous," "the Victorian Monstrosity": Sinclair McKay, *The Secret Lives of Codebreakers: The Men and Women Who Cracked the Enigma Code at Bletchley Park*, 31.

"irretrievably ugly," "lavatory-Gothic": McKay, *The Secret Lives of Codebreakers*, 33.

"inchoate, unfocused . . . to say indigestible": McKay, *The Secret Lives of Codebreakers*, 34.

"a nondescript provincial pile . . . of English towns": McKay, *The Secret Lives of Codebreakers*, 32.

"a dump": McKay, *The Secret Lives of Codebreakers*, 27.

"Before long . . . wooden huts": Gordon Welchman, *The Hut Six Story: Breaking the Enigma Codes*, 31.

"going around delivering . . . was inside them": McKay, *The Secret Lives of Codebreakers*, 28.

"You just assumed you'd be shot": McKay, *The Secret Lives of Codebreakers*, 52.

"I never even asked . . . told me anyway": McKay, *The Secret Lives of Codebreakers*, 55.

CHAPTER 19

"men of the professor type": John Simkin, "Government Code and Cypher School," Spartacus Educational, January 2020, https://spartacus-educational.com/GCCS.htm

"what you realize . . . it was marvelous": McKay, *The Secret Lives of Codebreakers*, 17.

"would be willing . . . in the event of war": Welchman, *The Hut Six Story*, 9.

"dashing good looks . . . sense of humor": David Kahn, *Seizing the Enigma: The Race to Break the German U-Boat Codes, 1939–1943*, 97.

"I was absolutely green . . . as quickly as possible": Welchman, *The Hut Six Story*, 31.

"For my part . . . former students": Welchman, *The Hut Six Story*, 84.

"was not enjoying being a stockbroker": Welchman, *The Hut Six Story*, 84.

"the four wicked uncles of Bletchley Park": "Gordon Welchman: Codebreaker," *Crypto Museum*, www.cryptomuseum.com/people/gordon_welchman.htm

"We treated . . . in cryptology": Kozaczuk, *Enigma*, 97.

"Herbstzeitlose . . . to attain eternity": Kozaczuk, *Enigma*, 97.

CHAPTER 21

"One of the first things . . . become invisible": Roger Steinway, "Interview: U-Boat Survivor's Story," HistoryNet, March 23, 2020, historynet.com/interview-u-boat-survivors -story.htm

"Good luck, Hans" "Look after yourself": Sebag-Montefiore, *Enigma*, 57.

"the consequent disadvantages . . . is too great": Sebag-Montefiore, *Enigma*, 59.

"Alarm": Sebag-Montefiore, *Enigma*, 62.

"He's got us": Sebag-Montefiore, *Enigma*, 63.

"Surface! Air in all the tanks": Kahn, *Seizing the Enigma*, 110.

"Abandon ship" "Blow her up! Report by radio": Kahn, *Seizing the Enigma*, 110.

"Herr Oberleutnant, I forgot to throw the wheels away": Sebag-Montefiore, *Enigma*, 66.

"looked like the gearwheel off a bicycle": Sebag-Montefiore, *Enigma*, 67.

CHAPTER 22

"Further advance . . . prisoners of war": F. H. Hinsley, *British Intelligence in the Second World War: Its Influence on Strategy and Operations, Vol. 1*, 336.

"happy brainwave": Kahn, *Seizing the Enigma*, 113.

"You won't be forgotten": Kahn, *Seizing the Enigma*, 113.

"Unbelievable! . . . Battle of Britain": Welchman, *The Hut Six Story*, 101.

"astonishingly bad habits": Welchman, *The Hut Six Story*, 98.

"called more for . . . experience at sea": Hinsley and Stripp, *Codebreakers*, 78.

"In keeping with . . . what I said": Hinsley and Stripp, *Codebreakers*, 78.

"I was and I remain . . . the loss of *Glorious*": Hinsley and Stripp, *Codebreakers*, 78.

"did all in its power . . . the Naval Section at Bletchley": Hinsley and Stripp, *Codebreakers*, 78.

CHAPTER 23

"The engineers . . . none of that": McKay, *The Secret Lives of Codebreakers*, 95.

"Bertrand's attitude . . . trying to obtain the machine": Turing, *X, Y & Z*, 150.

"Dear Menzies . . . A. G. Denniston": Turing, *X, Y & Z*, 144.

"I am resigned . . . so I accept it": Turing, *X, Y & Z*, 144.

"used for cheating in an examination": Welchman, *The Hut Six Story*, 78.

"some Eastern goddess . . . the oracle of Bletchley": McKay, *The Secret Lives of Codebreakers*, 93.

CHAPTER 24

"9th April. Thick fog. No wind": B. Jack Copeland, *Turing: Pioneer of the Information Age*, 58.

"Terrible sight . . . affected them so much": Copeland, *Turing*, 58.

CHAPTER 25

"an interesting example . . . expert examination": Alexander, *Cryptographic History of Work on the German Naval Enigma*, 24.

"Like a battery of knitting needles": Welchman, *The Hut Six Story*, 77.

"flashed into my mind . . . as I was": Welchman, *The Hut Six Story*, 81.

"W-I-R-H-O-F-F-E-N . . . we hope": Sebag-Montefiore, *Enigma*, 56.

CHAPTER 26

"One of our . . . help of others": Doenitz, *Memoirs*, 18.

"that it would . . . a secret": Doenitz, *Memoirs*, 22.

"the change [in strategy] caught us unawares . . . countermeasures had been prepared": Doenitz, *Memoirs*, 22.

"the U-boat will never again . . . in 1917": Doenitz, *Memoirs*, 23.

"for a naval officer . . . submarine warfare": Karl Doenitz, *Memoirs*, 23.

CHAPTER 27

"languages: none": Joe Miller, "Joan Clarke, Woman Who Cracked Enigma Cyphers with Alan Turing," BBC News, November 10, 2014, www.bbc.com/news/technology -29840653.

"the Prof": Hinsley and Stripp, *Codebreakers*, 114.

"enjoyable, not easy . . . a nervous breakdown": "Gendering Decryption—Decrypting Gender: The Gender Discourse of Labour at Bletchley Park, 1939–1945." Master's thesis, Uppsala University, 2013. uu.diva-portal.org/smash/get/diva2:625771/FULLTEXT01.pdf.

"was often so enthralling . . . over the workings": Hinsley and Stripp, *Codebreakers*, 117.

"lent me his alarm clock . . . at 2 A.M.": Hinsley and Stripp, *Codebreakers*, 114.

"The prospect of reading . . . another capture": Hinsley and Stripp, *Codebreakers*, 116.

CHAPTER 28

"cunning schemes" "pinch": Sebag-Montefiore, *Enigma*, 102.

"OPERATION RUTHLESS . . . English port": Sebag-Montefiore, *Enigma*, 102.

"preferred to work . . . Victoria Cross": Kahn, *Seizing the Enigma*, 125.

"Possibly Portsmouth area may be more fruitful": Sebag-Montefiore, *Enigma*, 103.

"like undertakers . . . Operation Ruthless": Sebag-Montefiore, *Enigma*, 103.

CHAPTER 29

"Everybody out": Sebag-Montefiore, *Enigma*, 84.

"The existence of any . . . is most unlikely": Sebag-Montefiore, *Enigma*, 87.

CHAPTER 30

"It was sunny . . . that is at its door": Paillole, *The Spy in Hitler's Inner Circle*, 154–157.

CHAPTER 31

"Soldiers of the western front! . . . a thousand years": Kozaczuk, *Enigma*, 104.

"long, drab building": Kozaczuk, *Enigma*, 105.

"Bei Durchfuehrung Paula . . . ueber Sedan": Kozaczuk, *Enigma*, 115. (Translation provided by Julia McCurdy.)

"Paula = Paris": Kozaczuk, *Enigma*, 115.

"he did not have . . . that number": Kozaczuk, *Enigma*, 107.

We have been defeated . . . Paris is open": Williamson Murray, "Churchill Takes Charge," HistoryNet, February 13, 2008, www.historynet.com/churchill-takes-charge.htm

"Where are the strategic reserves? . . . Aucune": Murray, "Churchill Takes Charge."

"Everything was falling apart . . . every man for himself": Paillole, *The Spy in Hitler's Inner Circle*, 167.

"It is a miracle . . . my Enigma": Paillole, *The Spy in Hitler's Inner Circle*, 167.

CHAPTER 32

"Suitcases cluttered . . . the fireplace": Paillole, *The Spy in Hitler's Inner Circle*, 166.

"You must leave France . . . too vulnerable": Paillole, *The Spy in Hitler's Inner Circle*, 168.

"When it was our turn . . . be insulted in England": Paillole, *The Spy in Hitler's Inner Circle*, 168.

"It was nearly midnight . . . to Morocco": Paillole, *The Spy in Hitler's Inner Circle*, 169.

"I have money . . . in Saint-Raphael": Paillole, *The Spy in Hitler's Inner Circle*, 169.

"confidential documents . . . counterfeiting paraphernalia": Paillole, *The Spy in Hitler's Inner Circle*, 169.

"a certain amount . . . his financial affairs": Paillole, *The Spy in Hitler's Inner Circle*, 17.

CHAPTER 33

"There is a traitor . . . running rampant among us": Paillole, *The Spy in Hitler's Inner Circle*, 183.

"Honor, common sense . . . honor and independence": "Charles de Gaulle Speech," BBC News, June 17, 2010, www.bbc.co.uk/news/10339678

CHAPTER 34

"with everybody killing . . . over the world": Nella Last, *The Diaries of Nella Last: Writing in War and Peace*, Friday, 14 February.

"cheese, eggs . . . practically unobtainable": Dimbleby, *The Battle of the Atlantic*, 126.

"grim-faced women . . . when served": Nella Last, *Nella Last's War: A Mother's Diary, 1939–1945*, 119.

"The only thing . . . the U-boat peril": Winston Churchill, *Their Finest Hour* [Adobe Digital Edition], 508/629.

CHAPTER 35

"all the guts in the world": Kahn, *Seizing the Enigma*, 132.

"They hauled me out": Kahn, *Seizing the Enigma*, 132.

"If it's locked . . . something there": Kahn, *Seizing the Enigma*, 135.

CHAPTER 36

"passing thought": Kahn, *Seizing the Enigma*, 154.

"Good God . . . mad moment": Kahn, *Seizing the Enigma*, 155.

"a series of short noises like a big alarm clock": Thomas Arthur Russell, "Approach of the Storm," BBC-WW2 People's War, November 25, 2005, bbc.co.uk/history/ww2peopleswar/stories/93/a7277493.shtml

"What's the name . . . *München*": Kahn, *Seizing the Enigma*, 158–159.

"One of our patrols . . . made prisoner": Kahn, *Seizing the Enigma*, 159.

"Organize a boarding party . . . you can find": Kahn, *Seizing the Enigma*, 163–164.

"a mischievous look . . . came ashore": Kahn, *Seizing the Enigma*, 163.

"At least I've got the cipher": Kahn, *Seizing the Enigma*, 168.

"I never thought we'd get any of this": Kahn, *Seizing the Enigma*, 168.

"Never mind . . . about this to anyone": Sebag-Montefiore, *Enigma*, 148.

"For God's sake . . . All this rubbish": Kahn, *Seizing the Enigma*, 180.

CHAPTER 37

"Here it is": Kahn, *Seizing the Enigma*, 181.

"It seems that . . . known to the enemy": Sebag-Montefiore, *Enigma*, 125.

"depressing event": Sebag-Montefiore, *Enigma*, 172.

"everything suggests . . . read our messages": Sebag-Montefiore, *Enigma*, 173.

"Our cipher does not appear to have been broken": Sebag-Montefiore, *Enigma*, 185.

CHAPTER 38

"it was doubted if the girls could do the work": McKay, *The Secret Lives of Codebreakers*, 101.

"The back of the machine . . . did not short": McKay, *The Secret Lives of Codebreakers*, 101–102.

"You had to be accurate . . . a short circuit": McKay, *The Secret Lives of Codebreakers*, 102–103.

"will not divulge . . . her own interests": McKay, *The Secret Lives of Codebreakers*, 103.

"There is nothing peculiar . . . highly commendable": McKay, *The Secret Lives of Codebreakers*, 104.

"How on earth . . . Something like that": Kahn, *Seizing the Enigma*, 138.

CHAPTER 39

"Five minutes . . . a third point, Welchman": Welchman, *The Hut Six Story*, 128.

"Sir, I would like to present . . . the Prime Minister" McKay, *The Secret Lives of Codebreakers*, 160.

"He stood rather uneasily . . . a cold wind": McKay, *The Secret Lives of Codebreakers*, 160.

"You all look very innocent . . . and never cackle": McKay, *The Secret Lives of Codebreakers*, 159.

"*Secret and Confidential* . . . P. S. Milner-Barry": Andrew Hodges, *Alan Turing: The Enigma*, 277–279.

"Make sure . . . this has been done": "Churchill's Action This Day Memo on Supply of Labour for Bletchley Park," The National Archives. https://images.nationalarchives.gov.uk/assetbank-nationalarchives/action/viewAsset?id=47277&index=261&total=396&view=viewSearchItem#

CHAPTER 40

"On February 1, 1942, the blow fell": Alexander, *Cryptographic History of Work on the German Naval Enigma*, 36.

"E bar 551 [the previous message] deciphers with setting B": Alexander, *Cryptographic History of Work on the German Naval Enigma*, 228.

"An average Shark . . . if possible": Alexander, *Cryptographic History of Work on the German Naval Enigma*, 36.

"the basic problem . . . few and far between": F. H. Hinsley, *British Intelligence in the Second World War: Its Influence on Strategy and Operations*, Vol. 2, 749.

CHAPTER 41

"Yesterday, December 7, 1941 . . . the Empire of Japan": Franklin D. Roosevelt, "The President Requests War Declaration 125," December 8, 1941.

"Hit them like . . . home empty-handed": Debi Blaney, "U-576: Life and Death on a World War II German U-Boat," NOAA Ocean Exploration and Research: Mission Logs

"The coast was not . . . deliver their attacks": Dimbleby, *The Battle of the Atlantic*, 249.

"the obvious defense . . . as usual": Dimbleby, *The Battle of the Atlantic*, 249.

"I greatly doubt . . . one would wish": Sebag-Montefiore, *Enigma*, 232.

"a mortal blow": Dimbleby, *The Battle of the Atlantic*, 23.

"All attempts to rescue . . . their crews": Dimbleby, *The Battle of the Atlantic*, 327.

CHAPTER 42

"You're not going. You're married": Sebag-Montefiore, *Enigma*, 240.

"Come on, Lacroix, it's your sub": Sebag-Montefiore, *Enigma*, 240.

"The lights were out . . . I took another lot up": Sebag-Montefiore, *Enigma*, 241.

"I saw Grazier . . . sink very quickly": Sebag-Montefiore, *Enigma*, 242.

"The seas were breaking . . . alongside the sea-boat": Sebag-Montefiore, *Enigma*, 242–243.

"What about the others? . . . I dived off": Sebag-Montefiore, *Enigma*, 242.

"on the run": Kahn, *Seizing the Enigma*, 226.

CHAPTER 43

"a little more attention . . . unless BP do help": Kahn, *Seizing the Enigma*, 217.

"It's out": Kahn, *Seizing the Enigma*, 226.

"It's come out in the zero position": Kahn, *Seizing the Enigma*, 227.

"I know all about it . . . well, congratulations": "It's Not a Welcome Memory. Two of Our Men Were Killed and I Nearly Died but We Did Capture the Vital Codes: Seizing the Enigma: Sole Survivor Tells of U-Boat Raid." The Free Library, June 12, 2000, https://www.thefreelibrary.com/It's+not+a+welcome+memory.+Two+of+our+men+were+killed+and+I+nearly . . . -a062672896

"Now however there were 70 bombes . . . a fascinating business": Alexander, *Cryptographic History of Work on the German Naval Enigma*, 52.

CHAPTER 44

"we would need a wheelbarrow to transport it": Paillole, *The Spy in Hitler's Inner Circle* 190.

"Really now . . . abandon that lead": Paillole, *The Spy in Hitler's Inner Circle*, 192.

CHAPTER 45

"Patron! . . . they're coming": Kozaczuk, *Enigma*, 138.

"We waited . . . more dead than alive": Kozaczuk, *Enigma*, 138.

"The harvest is good": Kozaczuk, *Enigma*, 138.

"The harvest . . . time for traveling": Kozaczuk, *Enigma*, 138.

CHAPTER 46

"You still say . . . shoot us": Turing, *X,Y & Z*, 235.

CHAPTER 47

"two young women . . . we were good friends": Kozaczuk, *Enigma*, 150.

"promised that he would . . . enter our compartment": Kozaczuk, *Enigma*, 150.

"found us at dusk . . . into the hands of the Germans": Kozaczuk, *Enigma*, 150.

"About three kilometers out . . . the first interrogation": Kozaczuk, *Enigma*, 156.

"I was expecting the worst . . . he said": Sebag-Montefiore, *Enigma*, 310.

"At that point I interrupted . . . they never came": Sebag-Montefiore, *Enigma*, 310–311.

CHAPTER 48

"He was speaking . . . right next to him": Paillole, *The Spy in Hitler's Inner Circle*, 201.

"I allowed myself . . . about the situation": Paillole, *The Spy in Hitler's Inner Circle*, 202.

"I hate and despise . . . Europe and its civilization": Paillole, *The Spy in Hitler's Inner Circle*, 202.

"connections . . . prepared to offer us": Paillole, *The Spy in Hitler's Inner Circle*, 203.

"Sequester Lemoine . . . in absolute secrecy": Paillole, *The Spy in Hitler's Inner Circle*, 203.

"I was expecting you tomorrow": Paillole, *The Spy in Hitler's Inner Circle*, 204.

"Lemoine spoke to me . . . be of assistance": Paillole, *The Spy in Hitler's Inner Circle*, 204.

"Lemoine has . . . no question of arrest": Paillole, *The Spy in Hitler's Inner Circle*, 205.

"I can no longer position myself . . . of the German authority": Paillole, *The Spy in Hitler's Inner Circle*, 205.

"Believe me . . . at the home of his mistress": Paillole, *The Spy in Hitler's Inner Circle*, 206–207.

"[Schmidt's] greed and venality . . . working for the Soviets": Paillole, *The Spy in Hitler's Inner Circle*, 208.

CHAPTER 49

"Be brave, my darling, be brave": Sebag-Montefiore, *Enigma*, 271.

"Cut the arm . . . for you": Sebag-Montefiore, *Enigma*, 271.

CHAPTER 50

"Go on—jump": Kozaczuk, *Enigma*, 205.

"Quelle aubaine pour les Anglais": Kozaczuk, *Enigma*, 207.

"Salve" "Amen": Sebag-Montefiore, *Enigma*, 286.

"Everything can still get better . . . meetings in Vichy": Paillole, *The Spy in Hitler's Inner Circle*, 220.

"Cdt. B. ist sofort . . . hat Ehrenwort gebrochen": Paillole, *The Spy in Hitler's Inner Circle*, 220.

"Rely on my . . . hide-and-seek with the Gestapo": Turing, *X,Y & Z*, 225.

"Michel has shaved off his moustache": Sebag-Montefiore, *Enigma*, 313.

"The spontaneous . . . masterfully played": Paillole, *The Spy in Hitler's Inner Circle*, 223.

EPILOGUE

"reached Admiralty . . . 19 minutes": Alexander, *Cryptographic History of Work on the German Naval Enigma*, 53.

"as ludicrous . . . using scientific methods": Paillole, *The Spy in Hitler's Inner Circle*, 224.

"The Hut 8 cryptologists . . . nothing but a headache": Alexander, *Cryptographic History of Work on the German Naval Enigma*, 51–52.

"there should be no question . . . it was Turing": Alexander, *Cryptographic History of Work on the German Naval Enigma*, 42.

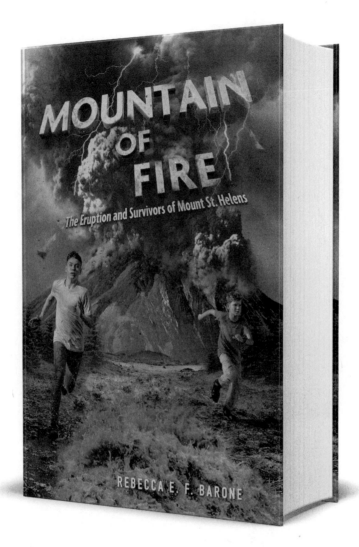

TURN THE PAGE FOR A SNEAK PEEK AT THE TRUE ACCOUNT
OF THE VOLCANIC ERUPTION OF MOUNT ST. HELENS,
THE STORY OF THE PEOPLE WHO DIED, THOSE WHO SURVIVED,
AND THE HEROES WHO FOUGHT TO RAISE THE ALARM.

PROLOGUE

THE MORNING WAS CALM, QUIET. THE SKY WAS CLEAR. FIVE AND a half miles in the distance, Mount St. Helens rose to a snow-covered peak.

Five and a half miles sounded far. Five and a half miles might seem like safety.

But David Johnston knew better. He knew volcanoes. He knew their speed. Five and a half miles, he knew, would never be enough.

Johnston was in the clearing, tending to the scientific instruments and radios, for one night only.

Maybe, he hoped, the mountain would stay quiet.

There was work to do. Measurements to take. Data to record. And, always, the mountain to watch. To be ready to raise the first alarm.

He was watching at 8:32 a.m.

Without warning, without a hint of noise, the side of the mountain fell away. The gray mass of roiling earth began tumbling, rolling down and away from the summit. A landslide that seconds later was followed by another.

Then, a blast. Darker, choppier.

Faster.

Johnston grabbed for the radio. He clicked it on. "Vancouver! Vancouver!" he said, breathlessly. "This is it!"

He clicked the microphone once more. And again.

Then, silence.

The gray, frothing blast swept toward him.

Five and a half miles would never be far enough.

MARCH 20–27, 1980

CHAPTER 1

59 DAYS BEFORE THE ERUPTION

THE THICK METAL CYLINDER TURNED SLOWLY. DAY AND NIGHT, it guided a long, narrow piece of paper moving faithfully underneath a quivering black pen. Day and night, the pen drew an unbroken, straight line.

Until 3:47 p.m.

Far underneath the surface of the earth, rock tore away from rock as a giant slab of the earth's crust wrested free from its trap. The earth trembled at the tear.

Miles above, the pen that had been steady a moment before jumped to life.

In a basement lab at the University of Washington in Seattle, Linda Noson was the first to notice. She knew as soon as she saw the dark marks streaking across the face of the paper: an earthquake. A big one.

Noson ran upstairs.

"We just got a four," she told Steve Malone, the head of the seismology lab. "From the Mount Rainier station."

Malone was up and out of his office the same moment. In the Pacific Northwest, there were thousands of earthquakes each year. But few reached as high as a magnitude 4.

The seismometer on Mount Rainer had registered the earthquake, but that didn't mean the center of the quake was anywhere near. Seismometers could detect movement of the earth's crust far from where the instruments were actually located. There had been an earthquake out there—somewhere—but where?

"I bet it's Mount Hood," said a student who had joined Noson and Malone.

"I'm thinking it's St. Helens," countered Malone, his intuition coming from years working around the mountains.

There was only one way to tell.

Noson was a seismic analyst, an expert in examining the lines and lurches of the recorder's pen. Straight or jagged, the recorder showed only a black path. Like all of science, it needed humans to translate the data into a meaningful story. Noson went to work.

Taking the paper, she noted times, locations, and magnitudes of movement. She went to her computer and wrote some code, walked a set of punch cards to the mainframe in another building, and waited while it slugged through the calculations.

"Steve's right," she said when she walked back into Malone's office. "It's Mount St. Helens."

A call to the Forest Service ranger station on Mount St. Helens confirmed it. Everyone there had felt the quake.

One earthquake—even a big earthquake—could be shaken off. One earthquake, alone, wasn't much to worry about.

As long as it was only one.

But over the night and into the next day, the earthquakes didn't stop.

It had been an ordinary, unremarkable Thursday afternoon when the first earthquake rolled the ground. Now the peace was broken.

Malone began to worry about avalanches. There was fresh snow on the ground, and Mount St. Helens was popular with mountain climbers. It might be time to get everyone off the mountain.

But when Malone called the avalanche forecaster to update him on the earthquakes, there was a different question weighing on the forecaster's mind. They all knew stories of how Mount St. Helens had erupted in the past. Ash had clogged the sky, turning bright day to black midnight. Pumice had rained down. Fire and lava had spewed from the summit. The Toutle River had become so hot that all the fish had died for miles around the mountain. It had happened barely more than a century before.

It could happen again.

"Is there going to be an eruption?" the forecaster asked.

"Well," Malone replied, "we don't know. But these earthquakes are continuing. So, sometime. Maybe. There could."

All weekend, the ground trembled and danced. "Sometime" seemed to grow closer every time the earth shook.

By Monday, Malone was beginning to panic.

Malone knew seismology. He knew the signs and signals of moving rock. What he didn't understand were volcanoes.

Luckily, he knew someone who did.

Dwight "Rocky" Crandell and his field partner Donal "Don" Mullineaux were volcanologists who had spent more than two decades studying Mount St. Helens with the United States Geological Survey (USGS). They had often traveled to Washington from their home base in Denver, Colorado, and they knew the mountain well. If something was about to happen, if Mount St. Helens was showing signs of erupting, they would know.

But when Malone first called Crandell to ask him for advice, Crandell's response was hardly what he was expecting.

"Don't worry. Don't worry, Steve," Crandell said. "The national [seismometer] network located it, and [the earthquake] is thirty kilometers [18.6 miles] away. Not a problem."

Malone was shocked.

"Woah! Rocky! Hang on. Wait a minute," Malone exclaimed. "We've got a station right at the volcano, on the west flank. And another one about fifty kilometers [31 miles] away . . . Our locations might be off by one or two kilometers [0.6 or 1.2 miles], but not thirty [18.6 miles]!"

Malone's instruments were much closer to Mount St. Helens than the USGS's network; after that first earthquake the week before, Malone had put seismometers *directly on* the mountain. Malone's instruments, and Malone's records, were the most reliable sources of information. To Crandell, the earthquakes appeared too far away for concern; to Malone, it seemed like Crandell was looking at bad data.

"There is no question," continued Malone, "that this earthquake is located directly under the volcano, slightly to the north of the summit, and at a very shallow depth!"

Slowly, Malone convinced Crandell that the earthquakes were indeed coming from Mount St. Helens. And they were coming faster and stronger every day.

"That got his attention," Malone remembered.

Crandell had a project in Denver that he couldn't leave, but his field partner, Mullineaux, was in Washington State the next day.

It was a good thing Mullineaux had come quickly, too. Because on Tuesday night, the earthquake activity increased tremendously. Noson had run up to Malone's office for a single magnitude 4 earthquake. Now, there were several magnitude 4 earthquakes *per hour.*

It's going somewhere, Malone thought to himself.

By Wednesday, the earthquakes were coming even faster. So many strong earthquakes, continuing for so many days, meant that something was going to happen.

"Well," said Malone, "the next day, it did."

CHAPTER 2

A KEG OF DYNAMITE

"IT SOUNDED JUST LIKE A SONIC BOOM," SAID FERROL FULLMER, who managed a hotel nearby.

At 12:58 p.m. on Thursday, March 27, 1980—one week after earthquakes had begun shaking the mountain—a plume of ash and steam shot seven thousand feet into the air from the top of Mount St. Helens.

On the ground, people stared up and wondered at the noise, but they couldn't see anything. Clouds covered the mountain's summit.

"People got on the roofs of buildings for a better view, but it just looked like a lot of black rain clouds," said Fullmer.

They heard the boom. They knew that the mountain had been shaking. But to people below the clouds, Mount St. Helens looked like it did any other day.

"There was no sign of molten lava," one newspaper reported, sounding somewhat frustrated.

Not only was there no lava, there was no surge of hot gases rushing down the mountainside. There were no mudflows cascading through the river. There was no ash falling like misplaced snow.

"Mount St. Helens, a lady with a 123-year-old tummyache," erupted with a gigantic volcanic burp," the *Spokesman-Review* wrote, condescendingly.

And just like a burp, the plume died off after it made some noise.

If this is what the earthquakes had been leading to, well, everyone was a bit disappointed. A loud "boom" . . . and that was it. A burp, even a big one, was hardly anything to get upset about.

The clouds made it especially easy to dismiss the steam blast. The only way to see the top of the mountain was to take to the air, and soon, the sky above the summit was full of planes.

It was exciting! It was thrilling! A volcano! There didn't *seem* to be any danger. The plume subsided after its initial eruption, and it was a beautiful day. Who wouldn't want to go see a once-in-more-than-a-hundred-years eruption?

"Dozens of light aircraft, filled with sightseers, journalists, geologists and even the governor—all eager for a peek at a real live volcano, flew through mostly clear skies [above the clouds] surrounding Mt. St. Helens Thursday afternoon," reported the *Spokesman-Review*.

Even Governor Dixy Lee Ray hadn't been concerned when she first heard about the eruption. In nearby Port Ludlow, she had been meeting with the judges of Washington State's Supreme Court when she was interrupted.

"I might just read you the note that has just been handed to me," she said, smiling. "We have received information that Mount St. Helens has erupted at 12:58 today," she continued. "I've always said, for many years, that I hoped I lived long enough to see one of our volcanoes erupt. Maybe I soon will get a chance."

She flew to Mount St. Helens that afternoon.

When her plane landed after circling the top of the volcano, she told the assembled reporters that "we could not see any steam or lava . . . from what we could see, everything is quiet now." Still, she agreed that "it was really quite a thrill."

To the audience in the sky, it seemed like the mountain-turned-volcano was the best event of the season—something to enjoy and not be scared of. But these were tourists. None of them had experience with volcanoes.

There was only one man in the sky that afternoon who had seen an eruption before. He had just happened to be in the area when the earthquakes had started; he had stayed to study what was coming next. David Johnston had a feeling that Mount St. Helens wasn't done yet.

Johnston was a volcanologist with experience in active volcanoes in Alaska. As a scientist for the USGS, he was usually based in California, but he had been attending a conference in Seattle when the earthquakes began. Over the past week, Malone had put Johnston to work deciphering seismic signals, but Johnston's specialty was volcanic gases. Now, with the mountain spewing steam and ash, he could really put his knowledge to work.

On the afternoon of the first blast from Mount St. Helens, Johnston stood in a clearing near the forest with his hands stuffed in his pockets. His shaggy, blond hair was caught under a blue knit winter hat, and his checkered flannel coat guarded him from the winter weather that still chilled the air in late March. An easy grin played across his face as he slouched and faced the reporters.

No one would've guessed that Johnston hated speaking in front of a crowd. He was so afraid of public speaking that, more than once, he had fainted while giving presentations.

But that fear paled next to the deal the reporters had offered: a view of Mount St. Helens from the sky, in exchange for an on-camera interview.

It was enough to make him smile, even in front of a crowd. Johnston swallowed his fear and climbed aboard the plane.

In the air, they followed the winding path of a river, over the old-growth forests blanketing the landscape below. While they flew beneath the clouds, bare, brown patches of ground were visible where the Weyerhaeuser Logging Company had harvested timber on some of the most profitable land in the country. Soon, though, Johnston and the news crew were rising above the clouds, finally catching sight of the top of the mountain.

The peak of Mount St. Helens, usually pristine with snow, was scarred with gray ash. As they drew closer, the ash resolved into cracks and crevasses, streaking down an otherwise blank, white mountain.

In the plane, every pair of eyes followed the gray lines up. There, at the top of the mountain, they saw it for the first time. A new crater.

"This is 335," one of the crew said over the radio, announcing their flight number before reporting what he saw. "I've got a bit of steam coming out of it, and I'd say it's probably about, uh, a twelve-hundred-foot crater. It's open at the very top of the mountain. About twelve-hundred feet by, about, oh, perhaps two hundred feet in the center."

Long gashes, like wounds in the earth from some terrified beast clawing at a nightmare, raked the ground next to the crater on the mountain top.

"We've got a crater," one of the crew said again. "It appears to just be slowly developing all across the top."

They circled Mount St. Helens and watched as a small landslide opened the crater a bit wider.

When they came down after the flight, the reporters asked: What did Johnston think? Were the plume of steam and the slowly growing crater the end of the mountain's drama, or was there more to come? The crowd of tourists in planes seemed to be having a good time, enjoying the spectacle from the air. But what was the real story?

Were the people of Mount St. Helens in danger?

"We're standing next to a dynamite keg and the fuse is lit," said Johnston. "I am genuinely afraid of it."

LATE MARCH–MAY 16, 1980

CHAPTER 3

THE ONE WHO SMOKES

JOHNSTON SHOULD *NOT* HAVE COMPARED THE MOUNTAIN TO A keg of dynamite. That was the last thing the US Geological Survey (USGS) needed: People were going to panic if they heard stories like that.

"We don't know how this will play out," a senior USGS scientist chided Johnston. "We don't want people in harm's way but [we] can't be fright merchants."

They were scientists, and their story should be grounded in theory, not guesses.

"There's really no good way to predict what will happen. No way," Don Mullineaux told reporters.

And no one knew the volcanic science of Mount St. Helens better than Rocky Crandell and Don Mullineaux.

The USGS monitored the country's volcanic hazards, and Mullineaux and Crandell were in charge of the Cascades, a mountain range in western North America. They were geologists who specialized in mapping previous eruptions. They'd used the records laid down in rock and dirt over centuries and millennia to weave a story of what had happened long ago.

"When I first met [Crandell]," Steve Malone remembered,

thinking back to years before when the two crossed paths around Mount St. Helens, "he was really fit looking, with all of his geology stuff hanging off of him . . . he had the holster for the rock hammer, and the notebooks, and the cameras . . . outfitted with all the gear."

Crandell, and Mullineaux with him, dug through layers of rock and soil, seeing how ash from previous eruptions changed the ground. They hiked over ridges and down valleys, searching to see how far each layer of ash stretched away from the mountain. They watched the trees and banks of the rivers. Where the Toutle River branched into the North Fork and the South Fork, they found that lahars—mudslides like thick cement containing everything from ice and dirt to trees and rocks moving as fast as 120 miles an hour—had flowed down each.

In their final report, Crandell and Mullineaux wrote that "Mount St. Helens has been more active and more explosive during the last 4,500 years than any other volcano in the conterminous United States."

"The volcano's behavior suggests . . . an eruption is more likely to occur within the next hundred years, and perhaps even before the end of this century," they concluded.